YOU NEVER DIE

BY
I.S. PETTEICE

I CAN FLY

PUBLICATION
CONSULTANTS
We Believe In The Power Of Authors

PO Box 221974 Anchorage, Alaska 99522-1974
books@publicationconsultants.com—www.publicationconsultants.com

ISBN Number: 978-1-59433-814-4
eBook ISBN Number: 978-1-59433-815-1

Copyright 2018 I.S. Petteice
—First Edition—

Manufactured in the United States of America

TABLE OF CONTENTS

FOREWORD

Religious faiths today would not dare associate the paranormal with religion. My familiarity of the paranormal began around age five; it may have been earlier. I did not ask for it. Perhaps it was inherited. I am told my great grandfather talked to the spirits. I would say that my father was psychic. He was also very religious. It was not something I practiced, nor did I attempt to follow in his footsteps. I did not even realize my father had psychic abilities until I was a teenager. For me, it was just there and I thought it was something everyone lived with – it was normal. That is, I thought it was something that everyone experienced until my mother told me to stop it; so, I learned not to say certain things around her that I thought might upset her. Not because I thought there was anything wrong, but because even at an early age I knew she did not like for me to talk about particular incidents.

I supposed it would be like a little child having what you believed to be an imaginary friend that he talks to and a parent telling him his friend is not really there. A parent will normally tell the child that they really are not seeing anything and they are a big girl or a big boy now and to stop talking to their imaginary friend, while the child really can see the friend, whether it be an angel or their spirit guide. At this time the angel or spirit guide will usually fade away as the child will no longer need their presence and the child will forget about them.

The difference is that psychic powers do not go away. They can be increased with use if the person is really aware of them, or they lessen somewhat when they are not used, but that intuitiveness stays. My father recognized my abilities and would share his ghost stories and travel encounters with me as I grew older. He did not encourage me, but he knew I was interested in his many narratives.

I believe paranormal relates or connects to religion because it embraces life beyond living on earth and if I can convince you of the paranormal, then if you are an atheist, or agnostic, or an unbeliever, perhaps you can become a believer that there has to be life beyond our living here and if you can believe that, you have to believe in a greater or higher power.

We are given free will by God. With that in mind, we can choose to have negative attitudes, or we can choose to have positive attitudes.

There was a little turtle that got tipped over onto his back. While watching the clouds go by overhead, and flailing his little legs, "Oh, my gawd," he exclaimed, "I'm flying."

I

OUT-OF-BODY EXPERIENCES, ASTRAL PROJECTION- TELEPORTATION, REMOTE VIEWING

I was zipping along, traveling very fast, not thinking about where I was going. Even though it was very dark, like a night without a moon, I could vaguely see huge buildings all along my right side that reminded me of an old western town. I suppose I could see them because I was light and the other spirits were light. The buildings seemed much larger than normal buildings would be and they were all connected. Or, maybe I just watch too many westerns on television.

As I traveled, I could catch glimpses of others spirits passing, going in the opposite direction, but we were all traveling so fast it was almost as though I felt them in contrast to really seeing them.

Maybe that wasn't it at all. Perhaps it was because we were all spirits and not in bodily form. I was in another dimension where I could travel without wings, just fly or zip about and go where I wanted to go, but not have to consciously think about it.

No one was communicating or attempting to communicate. Actually, I was being ignored. They were doing their thing and I was just enjoying flying around. I could have reached out and touched some of them, but we were spirits and there was no need to try. They were like lit, wispy, sheets flying by, and I did not know anyone. They were just whooshing by.

I don't know how I knew they were spirits, or how I knew I was a spirit. I just did. There didn't seem to be anything odd about it at the time.

When I woke up, I wanted to go there again because I remembered there was no pain. I was literally a light and I could fly about freely, but I did not remember having a destination, nor did I recall hearing any sounds. It was like a black void – a vacuum.

Later I read some place that it was not a dream but probably astral projection and that it is not uncommon for people to project at night while they are sleeping. In this state, you can go anywhere you choose to be at the speed of thought. An intuitive would call it lucid dreaming instead of astral projection because you are not awake while traveling. I would like to think if I was going to astral project I would choose to go someplace a little more pleasant – maybe somewhere not quite so dark – maybe a nice beach some place with a lot of sunshine. I've always liked sunshine.

Since that time, I have had one other out-of-body experience while sleeping. During that time my alarm clock went off just as my spirit was returning to my body. I was doing a hover over the top of my body and looking down at myself. I very clearly remember my eyes being open and I was looking down at my own body. I remember looking up at myself. I closed my eyes and I re-entered my body with a jolt as I, nor my body, was expecting to be awakened in such a manner. It was like one moment I was looking down at myself, and I blinked my eyes and I was back in my body. I was so surprised that I did not remember where I had been, or if I had been dreaming before returning to my body. I only remember hearing the alarm clock buzzing and seeing myself lying on the bed below me and then looking up and seeing myself above me.

That was many years ago and I am not consciously aware of having astral traveled since that time. Imagine hovering over your own body and seeing yourself from above and then having your own body below you open its eyes and look at you. It is like watching a dead body coming to life.

I believe we all do astral project quite often in our dreams. If you make a habit of recording your dreams you will be convinced there could be no other explanation for some of your dreams.

Quite often I have the same dream over and over where I visit the same two or three houses in a dream and in reality I do not know where the houses are and I wonder if I am astral traveling on those occasions?

Not convinced yet? There was one case reported of a woman that was struck by a hit-and-run driver on the highway. A stranger stopped to see if he could help her and she told him there was nothing he could do for her, but that if he was ever near where her mother lived, to tell her mother she was okay, happy, and already with her father. The stranger was so moved that he drove several hundred miles out of his way to deliver the message. What he found was that the victim's father had died of a heart attack just one hour before her being struck down.

Astral projection, or astral travel, is an out-of-body experience where the spiritual body leaves the physical body and travels in the spirit body into 'higher' dimensions. It is often reported in connection with dreams, and practices of different forms of meditation. There has never been any harm reported as a result from anyone astral traveling. Instead, the elimination of fear of death and the resolution of physical, mental, emotional and spiritual issues have been observed as a result of out-of-body experiences.

Anyone can practice having an out-of-body experience at will, and many people do. It takes a long time to learn as you have a fear of letting go of the safety of our bodies. Some psychic institutes have classes. I went to one class, but she got to the part about chakras and I didn't know what she was talking about and I got too distracted on that issue to get into leaving my body. I guess it was an advanced class and I didn't go back again. I was very frustrated because I really wanted to do it at the time.

The most important knowledge is to begin by being in a meditative or half-sleep state while lying in bed. You need to be very relaxed as if you are in a self-induced hypnotic state. You must be rested beforehand or you will just fall asleep. While you disassociate from your body, you start feeling as if you are floating and your mind shuts off from your physical body.

When you are ready, you envelop your physical body in a white light for protection. You see yourself completely surrounded by white light. There can be a great danger in leaving your body unguarded and traveling among spirits that are unfriendly. Some spirits would like nothing better than to inhabit an earthly body even if is not their own. I will talk about this later in this book.

When you let go of your body and lift, on your first few trips it is advisable to just move about in your own room, your immediate surroundings, until you are comfortable with leaving your body.

At this point, you can then pass through walls, windows, and go any place you choose to go. Go into town, go to a movie, go to the mall, go visit someone, go see Congress in action. That should hack your hackles. You could go see the pyramids; wherever you want to go, wherever you imagine yourself going. When you want to return, you think yourself back in bed, or back to your home. None of this can usually be achieved in the first attempt. It is not a natural experience and it is something that you have to allow your mind and body to adjust to. If you do not believe that you can astral travel, you will not be successful. A practiced traveler can travel to the other side of the world in a second. I could visit my sister 3,000 miles away in the blink of an eye and then return home and call her up and tell her what she was doing. Astral time is not the same as we know it.

I remember practicing and attempting to astral travel during one year. If I actually did succeed at traveling other than the two instances I have recounted here, I do not know it, because, during my practice efforts to travel, I always fell asleep because I was always tired when I tried.

A person is in an altered state of consciousness during an out-of-body experience. The one thing that is missing from this classification of distinguishing out-of-body experiences from a psychotic event, is the lucid nature of the experience. The out-of-body experience is a fairly common phenomenon since it occurs in 14-34% of the population depending on which study you look at. It would be ludicrous to say that up to one-third of the human population are mentally ill, when, in fact, this is such a common occurrence.

Additionally, think of the national security consequences.

Some astral travelers that were interviewed claim they can talk to their soul guides. Anyone that believes in life after death believes they have guides and angels that watch out for them. I can think of several times in my life when I was very near my soul guides, but we will also discuss that in a later chapter.

As an example, my father was a practiced traveler. He had a very bad heart and just walking from the house to the garage would cause him to have an angina attack, so his amusement was astral traveling. Mother just thought he was taking a nap. He always knew what I was doing unless I closed him out.

Mom and Dad raised us in a strict religious environment, and Dad was a Bible reader, so it always surprised me that he astral traveled and communicated with ghosts. I don't think he shared that information with the rest of the family.

With this in mind, after an unhappy seventeen-year marriage I got a divorce, but I did not tell my parents because they did not believe in divorce and no one in my family had ever gotten a divorce. Nearly a year after my divorce, I was talking to my father on the telephone, and he said, "I'm going to write you a letter and tell you something."

I immediately knew what he was referring to, so I said, "You send me a letter, and I'll write back and tell you if it is true or not."

My father sent me a letter and told me that he visited me and he said "You were sitting in a brown leather recliner, and you had papers scattered all around you. You had on a pink robe, and I think it was in April, and you looked up and you said 'I'm going to divorce Ned.'" (Name changed).

I was so relieved. I wrote back and told him "That is exactly how it happened." I explained that it was in April. I was sitting in the den in the recliner, in my pajamas and a pink robe, and I had all the bills spread out. I was going through them to see if I could afford to get a divorce and support myself. I then told him when I got the divorce and why. I also told him why I had not told them that I had gotten a divorce.

My father wrote back and told me how proud he was of me that I could go through something like that alone and stand on my own two feet and bounce back like I did.

There is something amazing about this kind of astral traveling that I believe needs to be explored further, and perhaps it is why it is not an effective science. My father could only visit if I was open and receptive to the idea. If he should call me up and say I am going to visit you tonight, and I did not want him to visit, I could close down, and he would not be able to visit. Or perhaps he could visit my home and just was not be able to find me. I'm not sure which. There is a privacy issue involved. Also, if a person has certain illnesses, they can no longer travel. Possibly that is because they might not want to return to their bodies. I believe God decides when you get to permanently leave your body.

To illustrate the point, the last time I saw my father alive he said, "Why can't I see you anymore?"

"Daddy, it is most likely because you are ill," I said.

Although he was very ill, I also wanted my privacy, and I shut down our connection. I suspect he could probably visit my home because he was a practiced traveler, but he just could not find me. Frankly, most of the time I did not know he was around unless he told me later. But it is like an invasion of privacy, someone peeping in your windows. I don't think he ever thought about it like that. I do not think a traveler ever does because they are a spirit at the time. But just because the person on the other end cannot see them does not make them any less intrusive.

So, if you decide to become a traveler, please remember that other people have privacy rights. You may want to go see what they are doing and think that is pretty cool, but they have a right to privacy so you should stay away unless it is agreeable to them that you visit. Otherwise, it is the same as breaking and entering, or being a peeping Tom, or voyeurism.

To summarize, an out-of-body experience is your mind, out-of-body, in an internally generated dream world. This does not mean your dreams literally take you out-of-body at night.

To clarify here is what separates an out-of-body experience from a typical dream:

1. You have a higher level of consciousness during the experience
2. You initiate the experience by exiting your perceived body

The first criteria means that to have an out-of-body experience you must be fully conscious, and you have vivid self-awareness during the experience. In this form, any type of lucid dream can represent an out-of-body experience.

The second criteria means that you are aware of leaving your body while it is lying in bed. You will begin in your bedroom, in the same position as your physical body. My father would astral travel while sitting in his recliner in the living room.

Another significant fact is that out-of-body experiences can be traced back to shamans that lived as long as twenty thousand years ago. There is a way to determine which dimension you have traveled on. There are five dimensions. Buddhists say there are seven dimensions. They refer to the first one as the Physical Plane and the last one as the Buddhaic plane.

THE ASTRAL PLANE – All buildings on this dimension appear immense in size and almost beyond description. Ghosts, telepathy, clairvoyance, and telekinesis, etc. (psychic phenomena) originate in this dimension. Quantum physics demonstrates that we live in a space-time continuum in which all events occur simultaneously. The Astral Plane has no time concept as we know it on Earth.

The astral plane is divided into lower and upper planes. The lower plane is for souls that have lived evil lives, and many would associate it with Hell. Catholics would describe it as purgatory. There is no spiritual growth there.

The upper astral plane is a more beautiful and desirable dimension. For most people, the soul goes here following physical death.

The roar of the sea is the sound characteristic of this dimension.

THE CAUSAL PLANE – The causal plane is the location of our Akashic records. The Akashic records are a detailed account of all our past, present, parallel and future lives. The progression of our soul's spiritual growth is reflected in these records. Every thought, everything you ever did is contained in these records. These records may be accessed while on any other plane.

The tinkling of bells can be heard when you tour this dimension.

THE MENTAL PLANE – The "Aum" or "Om" sound originates here.

On the mental plane thought, philosophy, ethics, moral teaching and intellectual functions dominate. Masters on the physical plane (Jesus, Buddha, etc.) did their work here during their waking state when they occupied a physical body. Most of the time these and current day Masters are out of the physical body and residing on the mental plane.

The sound of running water is heard on this plane.

ETHERIC PLANE – Truth and beauty are the most significant lessons our soul learns on the etheric plane. This plane is the source of our subconscious and primitive thoughts. This dimension appears flat to the soul traveler due to its vast size. Brilliant white lights dominate the sky of this plane, and the sound of buzzing bees is heard continuously.

THE SOUL PLANE – The soul plane is the ultimate destination of the soul upon its death. It is from here that we eventually ascend. It is here where Spiritualists believe our Higher Self and Masters and Guides educate us and assist us in the selection of our next lifetime.

The sound of a single note from a flute is characteristic of this plane.

A person in the Casual Plane that visits the Akashic records can get a glimpse of their own future and perhaps effect a minor change in their future to avoid an accident. For instance, you might see that you will have an accident on your way to visit a friend tomorrow. You can affect a minor change by changing the date or time you make your visit, thus avoiding the accident.

Carrington, Muldoon, Peterson, and Williams claim that the subtle body is attached to the physical body using a psychic silver cord. The final chapter of the Biblical Book of Ecclesiastes is often cited in this respect: "6. Or ever the silver cord be loosed, or the golden bowl be broken, or the pitcher be broken at the fountain or the wheel broken at the cistern. '7. Then shall the dust return to the earth as it was: and the spirit shall return unto God who gave it."

II Corinthians 12:1-4 may also refer to an out-of-body experience when it says: "12 It is not expedient for me doubtless to glory. I will come to visions and revelations of the Lord. 2 I knew a man in Christ above fourteen years ago, (whether in the body, I cannot tell; or whether out of the body, I cannot tell: God knoweth;) such a one caught up to the third heaven. '3 And I knew such a man, (whether in the body, or out of the body, I cannot tell: God knoweth;) '4 How that he was caught up into paradise and heard unspeakable words, which it is not lawful for a man to utter."

Soul travel appears in various other religious beliefs. For example, ancient Egyptian teachings present the soul as having the ability to hover outside the physical body in the Ka or subtle body.

There are many stories of the Prophet Mohammad's out-of-body experiences, as well as the Chinese Taoists, and the Yogis of India.

Likewise, in Japanese mythology, an ikiryō is a manifestation of the soul of a living person separately from their body. Traditionally, if someone holds a sufficient grudge against another person, they believe that a part, or the whole, of their soul can temporarily leave their body and appear before the victim of their hate in order to curse or otherwise harm them, similar to an evil eye.

In the Amazon, the yaskomo of the Waiwai is believed to be able to perform a "soul flight" that can serve several functions such as healing, flying to the sky to consult cosmological beings to get a name for a new-born baby, flying to the cave of peccaries' mountains to ask the father of peccaries for abundance of game, or flying deep down in a river to get the help of other beings.

Emanuel Swedenborg was one of the first soul travelers to write comprehensively about the out-of-body experience in his Spiritual Diary (1747–65). French philosopher and novelist Honoré de Balzac's fictional work "Louis Lambert" suggests he may have had some astral or out-of-body experience.

There are many twentieth century publications on astral projection, although the few authors widely cited are Robert Monroe, Oliver Fox, Sylvan Muldoon and Hereward Carrington, and Yram.

American, Harold Klemp, who is the current Spiritual Leader of Eckankar, practices and teaches Soul Travel through contemplative techniques known as the Spiritual Exercises of ECK (Divine Spirit).

There is no scientific evidence that astral projection as an objective phenomenon exists, and pseudoscientific claims to that effect are not accepted as reliable scientific evidence in the relevant fields of study.

Another closely related phenomenon is Remote Viewing. Remote Viewing is seeking impressions about an unseen distant target using extrasensory perception or "sensing with the mind." There is no credible scientific evidence that remote viewing works. The topic of remote viewing has been described as pseudoscience. In early occult and spiritualist literature, remote viewing was known as telesthesia.

"Remote viewing was popularized in the 1990s upon the declassification of certain documents related to the Stargate Project, a $20 million research program that had started in 1975 and was sponsored by the U.S. government, in an attempt to determine any potential military application of psychic phenomena. The program was terminated in 1995 after it failed to produce any useful intelligence information." http://en.wikipedia.org/wiki/Remote_viewing

Similarly, in 1973, Stanford Research Institute conducted a project referred to as "The Jupiter Probe." The purpose was to have subjects attempt to "remote view" Jupiter before NASA's Pioneer 10 Spacecraft flew past with its cameras. One of the viewers, Ingo Swann, was able to describe Jupiter just as the spacecraft cameras were able to see it a few weeks later.

In 1995, the CIA hired the American Institutes for Research to perform a retrospective appraisal of the results generated by the Stargate Project. Reviewers included Ray Hyman and Jessica Utts. Utts maintained that there had been a statistically significant positive effect, with some subjects scoring 5%–15% above chance. Hyman argued that Utts' conclusion that ESP had been proven to exist, "is premature, to say the least." Hyman said the findings had yet to be replicated independently, and that more investigation would be necessary to "legitimately claim the existence of paranormal functioning." Based upon both of their studies, which recommended a higher level of critical research and tighter controls, the CIA terminated the $20 million project in 1995. Time magazine stated in 1995 that three full-time psychics were still working on a $500,000-a-year budget out of Fort Meade, Maryland. David Goslin, of the American Institute for Research, said, "There's no documented evidence it had any value to the intelligence community." http://en.wikipedia.org/wiki/Remote_viewing.

As well, remote viewing is something everyone can do since we are all multi-dimensional beings. It is simply moving our consciousness from one location to another. You could describe it as using your third eye to see something in the next room or another location. In remote viewing, you could focus on a piece of paper sealed in an envelope or something written on a chalkboard in the next room. Remember when Johnny Carson used to perform Carnac, The Magnificent, by drawing an envelope from a mayonnaise jar and holding the envelope up to his forehead? Ed McMahon would say something like "Rose Bowl," and Johnny would reply, "What do you say when it's Rose's turn at the bowling alley?"

Another equally important experience is Teleportation, which is the process of physically relocating the body from one place to another site without touching it in anyway. What we find in a true teleportation is that the physical body dematerializes (disappears) from one location and subsequently rematerializes (reappears) in a different spot in an instant often accompanied by a "pop" sound. Sound impossible?

Teleportation, also known as time travel, is not the same as an out-of-body experience. An out-of-body experience is moving the soul from one dimension to another. Teleportation is the movement of the entire body from one location to another. If you could witness someone teleporting, you would see them slowly disappear. The person undergoing teleportation would experience an increase in their energy vibrating at high speed, accompanied by a tingling, buzzing sensation and/or feeling of spiraling upward. When you teleport, your body travels at the speed of light.

If you have a computer and google teleportation, you will find videos of actual teleportations.

Teleportation can be attempted in three ways:

(1) The first is spontaneous. Perhaps you were performing a particular chore you had carried out many times previously and for just a second you had the feeling you were someplace else. Or perhaps you were going someplace and suddenly realized you had traveled much further from your origin than was possible in the time you had been walking or driving.
(2) You have been teleported during a sleep state. This means your physical body has been teleported to another dimension. Your memory is very clear, and you recall physical sensations.
(3) A consciously directed teleportation. Teleporting takes practice for accuracy because at first, you will probably not end up where you wanted to go since your body travels at the speed of light. When you return to your body, you will again hear a "pop" sound.

In order to teleport, your mind has to block out all distractions. Only your limiting beliefs will prevent you from experiencing this distinctive form of travel. You will find it easiest to teleport at night because your body has had many spontaneous teleportation experiences while dreaming. You should teleport to secluded places to avoid shocking others when you materialize in front of them.

Most people do not remember their dreams, but with a little practice, you can. Every night before you go to sleep, tell yourself you will remember your dreams. In 3 or 4 days, you will wake up and find yourself reviewing a dream you just had or perhaps several dreams you had during the night. As you develop, you will be able to determine which ones are dreams and which are out-of-body experiences.

A dream is a stream of thought taking place while you are asleep. Freud believed that dreams are a window into our unconscious, and perhaps he was correct. Dreams are subjective sensations that we may or may not remember, that we experience while we are asleep. Maybe a dream is about someone you know or someone you don't know. Maybe you are someplace you have been before, or someplace completely foreign to you. Maybe it is a dream you have had before. Dreams also have meanings and there are sites on the internet where you can go to find out the meaning of your dream.

By showing different dimensions and being able to remove the spirit from the body, we are revealing life after death.

Teleportation is not something new. Read Acts 8:26-28 where it says, "26 And the angel of the Lord spake unto Philip, saying, Arise, and go toward the south unto the way that goeth down from Jerusalem unto Gaza, which is desert. 27 And he arose and went: and, behold, a man of Ethiopia, a eunuch of great authority under Candace queen of the Ethiopians, who had the charge of all her treasure, and had come to Jerusalem for to worship, 28 Was returning, and sitting in his chariot read Esaias the prophet." Was this teleportation?

In Acts 8:38-40, "38 And he commanded the chariot to stand still: and they went down both into the water, both Philip and the eunuch; and he baptized him. 39 And when they were come up out of the water, the Spirit of the Lord caught away Philip, that the eunuch saw him no more: and he went on his way rejoicing. 40 But Philip was found at Azotus: and passing through he preached in all the cities, till he came to Caesarea. "Phillip is teleported about 30 miles after baptizing the Ethiopian Eunuch.

In the book of John, Chapter Six, verses Sixteen through Twenty-One: "16 And when even was now come, his disciples went down unto the sea, 17 And entered into a ship, and went over the sea toward Capernaum. And it was now dark, and Jesus was not come to them. 18 And the sea arose by reason of a great wind that blew. 19 So when they had rowed about five and twenty or thirty furlongs, they see Jesus walking on the sea, and drawing nigh unto the ship: and they were afraid. 20 But he saith unto them, "It is I; be not afraid." 21 Then they willingly received him into the ship: and immediately the ship was at the land whither they went."

Jesus not only teleported himself three or four miles to the shore, but the boat and the disciples in the boat as well. When the disciples questioned him about it, he called it a miracle.

Of course, scientists say it is impossible. They believe we need to first teleport something to where we want to go – a landing pad of sorts. Then we need to disassemble our trillion, trillion atoms in our body and send them to that landing pad and then reassemble them on the landing pad.

Sounds to me like there is something beyond this life.

One night I left a place where I had been playing pool. I entered my car around 11:00 p.m. I had nothing to drink of an alcoholic nature. I do not remember anything else until some time later when I was sitting at a stop light in a left turn lane about four miles down the road. I became disoriented because I did not know where I was, nor how I got there. I assumed since I was in the left turn lane that I was supposed to turn left when the light turned green. Everything was pitch black outside, except for the red stop lights on each corner. I looked around for street signs and found the one going East, the direction I was pointed, but I did not see one for the direction I was going to turn. I decided to go ahead and turn the corner and drive until something looked familiar. Was I teleported those four miles, or did I have a moment of senility at age 38?

II

NEAR DEATH EXPERIENCES (NDE'S)
(The Next Dimension)

A Near Death Experience (NDE) is any experience in which someone close to death or suffering from some trauma or disease that might lead to death, perceives events that seem to be impossible, unusual or supernatural. It is the reported memory of all impressions during a special state of consciousness. There are many books on the subject.

How many times have you heard the expressions "my whole life flashed before my eyes," or "they're at the brink of death," or "go to the light"? You have probably heard someone say it; perhaps someone in your family. Or perhaps you heard the dialogue in a movie.

My research has turned up thousands of testimonies of Near Death Experiences. And they are not just recent. Plato's "Republic," written in 360 B.C.E. contains the tale of a soldier named Er, who had a Near

Death Experience after being injured in battle. Er described his soul leaving his body, being judged along with other souls and seeing heaven.

Also, many physicians and psychiatrists have done research on Near Death Experiences. Their research encompassed thousands of patients from many different cultures and religions.

P.M.H. Atwater, L.H.D. stated that in her research "Around eighty percent of the people who experienced near-death states claimed that their lives were forever changed by what happened to them. On closer examination, however, a pattern of surprising dimensions emerged. Experiencers were not returning with just a renewed zest for life and a more spiritual outlook. They were evidencing specific psychological and physiological differences on a scale never before faced by them. And this was true with child experiencers, as well as with teenagers and adults."

It appeared that no matter what culture or religion, there were several common denominators in all of the cases;

(1) At the moment of death, when you leave the physical body, there is a total absence of pain, fear or anxiety;

(2) You are totally aware of the environment where the death occurred;

(3) You are aware of any resuscitative attempts, or if you are in an accident, you are aware of the people attempting to rescue you; and

(4) Nearly all patients return with a sense that everything in the universe is connected. You are part of everything, and everything is a part of you. This is all usually observed from a few feet away.

Furthermore, this also occurs at a time when there is no measurable brain activity. It happens when a physician finds no sign of life whatsoever.

Yolaine Stout, President of The American Center for the Integration of Spiritually Transformative Experiences, said that one-third of Americans has had some form of a spiritual awakening. Also, she said that "There is research that shows up to 50 percent of these people suffer from some form of depression unable to integrate their spiritual experience with the very material experience of modern life. Many of these people are instead of being overjoyed in knowing there is a great love in eternity are angry. They are angry being trapped in an unloving world when they know there is another realm that is so different, so caring, so giving, so accepting."

Also, this new body – this ethereal body, is where you will be whole again. If you ever had an arm or leg cut off, you will now have it back again. Whether you were blind or deaf, you can now hear, see, talk, dance, and sing. If you were an MS patient bound in a wheelchair from paralysis, now you can sing and dance again. There is no pain, and there are no handicaps. Wow! And to think it is a sin to commit suicide.

The question came up among many physicians as to whether this was wishful thinking where anyone that had been in pain, or perhaps an MS patient, just looked forward to a time when their suffering would end. Very old people get that attitude. But in the cases of Near Death Experiences researched, many of the cases were sudden, unexpected accidents. One case was reported of a man that was in an accident where both of his legs were amputated while he was driving along a highway, yet he was aware of having both legs on his ethereal body that is perfect in every way. He could not have had previous knowledge that he was going to lose his legs.

Also, important to note is that research also included several blind people. When questioned about their experiences, the blind person could give intimate details of the people around them, including the color and type of clothing they wore; details a blind person would not otherwise be able to give.

Although NDEs are normally reported as a result of vehicle accidents, they also occur from asthma attacks, heart attacks, high fevers, drug overdoses, or drownings only to name a few. Some have been reported as a result of a dream.

Indeed, there will always be unbelievers and skeptics. There are thousands that have had near death experiences and to them, they have already met God and were sent back to this time because their life experience on earth was not yet finished. To those people, there is life after death.

Not surprisingly, you would hear more about this subject, but society prevents NDEs from sharing their experiences. We tend to label, belittle, or deny stories that do not fit into our model.

On the whole, most Near Death Experiencers (NDEs) share some common traits such as seeing very bright, or pure, or white lights. Some NDEs describe the light either as heaven or God. Another commonality is the out-of-body experience (OBE). The subject/patient/person (now a spirit) feels he has left his body and can look down at him/her body and others in the room and can later describe what is taking place --- usually, the doctors working on him/her. At this time, the "spirit" at times flies off into the sky and sometimes elsewhere. Near-death experiencers and some out-of-body experiencers can glimpse a world held together by unconditional love as a matrix for communication, a way of life, and total knowledge. The "spirit" according to his faith will enter into another realm or dimension, whether Heaven or Hell.

During the Out of Body Experience, the Spirit will encounter "beings of light" or other representations of spiritual entities that he will perceive as deceased loved ones, saints, or God.

Also, many spirits (NDEs) when leaving their body tell of going through a tunnel with a light at its end. Some speak of encountering spirit beings as they pass through the tunnel.

Before the Near-Death Experience ends, many spirits report a strong communication with a spirit being which is often expressed as a "strong male voice" telling them it is not their time and to go back to their body.

Some get to choose between going into the light or returning to their earthly body. Others feel compelled to return by a voiceless command, possibly by God.

Finally, some may even recall receiving a life review. He may perceive some form of judgment by a spirit entity they believe is Jesus.

As a result, these events become a totally life-changing experience for the individual. Many never previously believed in life after death. A few never previously believed in God.

A Near Death Experience and an Out-of-Body Experience (OBE) is not the same thing and has nothing to do with each other. An Out-of-Body Experience has nothing to do with death or dying but still may have spiritual elements and feelings of calm. Out-of-Body Experiences can happen spontaneously or can happen through meditation or even be drug induced.

One of the most moving Near-Death Experiences I have read about is that of Carter Mills. "In 1979, Berkley Carter Mills made history in the Commonwealth of Virginia by becoming the youngest father ever to win custody of a small child in divorce proceedings. Six months later a massive load of compressed cardboard he was loading slipped out of control, slamming him against a steel pole. He remembers a sharp pain, collapsing, being in a black void, then finding himself floating in a prone-position, twelve feet above his crumpled body. He saw and heard people running around, yelling for an ambulance and saying, "Don't touch him, give him air." His body went from white to blue; there was no breath. The sight filled him with awe. "I'm here; my body is there. How did this happen?" (Refer to pages 72-75, paperback version, *"Beyond The Light."*)

'Not understanding how he could suddenly be airborne, Carter Mills attempted to re-enter his body. Crawling downward in swim-like strokes he had almost reached his goal when a gentle but firm hand tugged his right arm. When he looked up, there were two angels replete with robes, wings, bare feet, and streaming hair - no color but opaque white - and no particular gender. "What's going on?" he asked. "We've come to take you to God," they answered. After some confusion on Carter Mills' part, the trio left the scene at tremendous speed, leaving the earth behind as if it were a star the size of a pinhead.

'Their destination was an intensely bright light. Carter Mills questioned, "How come I'm not cold and how come I'm not suffocating this far out in space?" An angel replied, "This is your spiritual body, and these things do not affect it." They took him to a suspended platform, and in the center was a being so powerful Carter Mills thought it was God. The angels bowed and took their places with two others, each with wings outstretched and hands folded in prayer, at the platform's four corners. Male in mannerisms and voice, the clean-shaven being, turned out to be Jesus.

'Carter Mills could not look Jesus in the face as he perceived himself as naked and unfit for such an audience. After some coaxing from Jesus, he felt more at ease. "I'm going to judge you," Jesus said. Instantly Carter Mills' whole life began to play out, starting at birth. He relived being a tiny spark of light traveling to Earth as soon as egg and sperm met and entering his mother's womb. In mere seconds, he had to choose hair color and eyes out of the genetic material available to him and any genes that might give him the body he would need. He bypassed the gene for clubfootedness; then he watched from a soul's perspective as cells subdivided. He could hear his parents whenever they spoke and felt their emotions, but any knowledge of his past lives dissolved. The birth was a shock: awful lights, giant people, eyes peering over face masks. His only comfort was his mother.

'He relived each incident in his life, including killing a mother bird when he was eight. He was so proud of that single shot until he felt the pain the bird's three babies went through when they starved to death without her.

"It's not true that only humans have souls," Carter Mills cautions today. "Insects, animals, plants have souls, too. Yes, I still eat meat, for in this plane species eat each other to survive, but I bless my food and say thanks for the gift life gives. If I don't the food sours in my stomach."

'He was shown that hell is a black blankness without God. Upset, he yelled back, "How can you sit up here on this throne and allow such misery to happen on Earth?" Gently he was told, "It's your fault. I gave you the tools to live by. I gave you free will and free choice. And I allow you to be part of my creation. It is your free will and your free choice that is responsible for starvation, war, and hate." Carter Mills felt pangs of guilt when he realized we coexist with God; no one is God's servant or slave.

'Jesus, the angels, and platform disintegrated into a giant sphere of light once Carter Mills no longer needed their shape or form to put him at ease. As the sphere grew it absorbed him, infused him with the ecstasy of unconditional love. "Sexual orgasms can't compare. You are so high. Magnify that to infinity!" He zoomed back to his mangled remains as a ball of all knowing light and crashed into his solar plexus with such force it jolted his body to action. He had been told before leaving The Other Side, "No hospital, no blood, no operation, God will show you how to heal yourself." Thus, when Carter Mills stood, he promptly walked to his car and drove home, on the way passing the ambulance that had been sent to rescue him. Those present verified that he had been dead for twenty minutes. The next morning Carter Mills awoke in a pool of blood.

'The doctor he went to for aid committed him to a psychiatric ward as insane when he refused surgery. Since three independent psychiatrists had to confirm the verdict, and one objected, Carter Mills was released. Although his injuries were extensive and severe, he recovered by himself and returned to work. His former wife took advantage of his plight and challenged the custody ruling three times. She lost each try.

"'The authorities tried to take my son away. I lost half my friends, my job, almost everything else I had, but I didn't lose God's guidance. I wouldn't talk about my experience for two years. I went from an active social life to that of a cripple before I could change things. I wanted to get a degree in psychology but had to quit several years later when my money ran out."

'Carter Mills' appearance on the Geraldo Show in 1989 was preceded by an old buddy breaking off their friendship just because he had agreed to discuss his near-death experience on national television. Carter Mills was heartbroken, yet appear he did, there and hundreds of other places, sharing the voluminous knowledge he was given while on The Other Side. For this, he has been hated and thanked, shunned and welcomed. His mind is often flooded with incredibly accurate prophesies that leave him frustrated for want of knowing what to do about them. Sometimes he feels as if he's losing personal control. Light bulbs even blow up in his presence if he flips on/off switches too fast. Nonetheless, he is now healthier than ever, youthful and energetic, and he brags about how his son has turned out in spite of all the problems. 'My sacrifices were worth it, for my son knows that God is real. He is drug-free and tuned to his own soul.'" http://www.iands.org/nde-stories/17-nde-accounts-from-beyond-the-light.html

If we are to believe Carter Mills, before our birth we decide ourselves what our future is going to be. We decide what kind of life we are going to live... whether we are going to be short, tall, fat, skinny, crippled or perhaps we have downs syndrome. We decide what lessons we want to learn in this life and the appearance of our outer shell helps us in learning those lessons.

It is interesting to note that people that think they are attractive believe they belong to a relatively higher social class wherein people that do not think they are attractive generally believe they belong to a lower social class. Physical attractiveness usually earn substantially more.

Research also finds that people's beliefs about their physical appearances influence their attitudes toward equality. When they thought they were more attractive, they became more supportive of inequality.

Certainly, how children are brought up and the environment in which they are raised makes a difference in their personality. Probably the most influential and discernable factor that influences environment is your physical appearance. This would tip the scale the heaviest in the nature-nurture debate

It is not always a matter of social impact of a physical disability as whether the disabled can accept their own disability. Society accepts people for who they are, but individuals have a difficult time accepting their own inadequacies.

In 2011, Alexander Wutzler of Berlin, Germany suggested that near-death experiences could be triggered by an increase of serotonin in the brain. Charles Q. Choi in an article for the Scientific American concluded, "scientific evidence suggests that all features of the near-death experience have some basis in normal brain function gone awry." People who had experienced times when their brains behaved as if they were dreaming while awake are more likely to develop the near-death experience.

While Kenneth Ring, a professor of psychology, has identified a set of value and belief changes associated with people who have had an NDE. These changes include a greater appreciation for life, higher self-esteem, greater compassion for others, a heightened sense of purpose and self-understanding, desire to learn, elevated spirituality, greater ecological sensitivity and planetary concern, and a feeling of being more intuitive. For some, these changes have also included increased physical sensitivity; diminished tolerance of light, alcohol, and drugs; and a feeling that one is now using the "whole brain" rather than a small part.

There are many debates on whether Heaven is real. The atheist totally believes there is no God; when you die that is the end. But a person having an NDE, even one that previously was an atheist, has no doubt of life after death and there being a Heaven and a Hell. There are many best-selling books and videos on the market by people that have had Near Death Experiences, and they all state that we have a life in eternity. Even some coma patients that have been interviewed stated that they have had some of the same uniqueness and commonalities in their adventures.

So, is a near death experience a hallucination, spiritual experience, or proof of life after death? Or, as some scientists would say, is it just a chemical change in the brain before death? Many people every day die for several minutes from automobile accidents, drowning accidents, heart attacks and other traumatic events only to be revived or return to their bodies much later when they should be braindead or unable to live a normal life and be able to tell what was happening around their earthly body while they were gone, but tell a phenomenal story of other events that took place in space and heaven.

III

GHOSTS-BANSHEES

I was just a skinny little seven-year-old kid that was suddenly awakened in the middle of the night. I have no idea what woke me up. I heard the back door open between the kitchen and the front porch, but that was after I was awake. I then heard the door between the kitchen and living room open and close. I kept listening and I was wondering why I did not hear any footsteps. Somehow, I instinctively knew he was coming to my room. I did not understand why, or what was happening, and I was becoming more and more fearful. I intuitively knew who it was and that he was making his way towards my room.

It was a hot summer night. No one heard of air conditioning back in the forties. They didn't even have electric fans in those days that I knew about, or at least we didn't have one. In the summer time you just left your windows open and hoped for a nice breeze so you could get some sleep. If you were among the more fortunate, you had screens on the windows to keep the mosquitos out. When you went in and out the doors during the day you hoped the flies and mosquitos didn't come in.

I always hated the sound of a buzzing mosquito in my bedroom after dark. You covered up with a sheet whether it was hot or not because you always knew that mosquito was going to get you. I can remember mom always had a sticky fly catcher dangling from someplace in the kitchen.

My heart was pounding in my throat and I could hardly breathe. I quickly pulled the sheet up over my head and I laid as still as I could. I tried to hold my breath so it wouldn't look like anyone was in my bed. Even though I knew who it was, and I don't know how I knew, by the same token, at my young age I saw no reason for a visit from him in the middle of the night. After what seemed like an eternity, I slowly pulled the sheet down to my nose and peeked out. Sure enough, there he was, still standing, dressed in his suit, at the foot of the bed, just staring at me.

Why? Why was he there? How did he know where I was -- which room I was in? Why was he staring at me? Not knowing what else to do, I pulled the sheet back over my head and tried to hold my breath, thinking, "please, just go away!" I kept my head covered up until I heard the kitchen door open and shut again.

The next morning Mom was combing and braiding my hair in the living room, and I said, "Mom, Brother Evans came to visit me last night."

Mother yanked at my hair and snapped, "Oh," with that scolding inflection only mothers can get in their voice when they are agitated with you. "Stop saying things like that. You know that isn't true. What makes you talk like that anyway?"

But, it was only a very short time later, perhaps five minutes -- at least in kid time -- there was a knock on the door. It was two ladies from church.

"Come in," mom said.

"Oh, we can't stay," one of the ladies said. "We just came by to tell you that Brother Evans died last night."

I find it interesting that (1) Brother Evans felt the need to say goodbye to this little kid before he departed this life. I remember all the kids at church going to their house for an Easter egg hunt and Brother Evans got a kick out of helping me find some Easter eggs. I remember the last egg he helped me find was in the ash bin compartment of the old coal stove in their living room. He kept telling me I was getting warmer, or colder, until I found it. (2) Why did I hear the back door open and close and no one else in the house did? He had to pass mom and dad's bedroom before getting to mine. (3) I do remember recognizing that it was him standing at the foot of the bed. I did not think at that age that he was an apparition. And I knew it was him when he was coming in the house. (4) Why couldn't I hear any footsteps? (5) Why did I wake up in the middle of the night in the first place?

Ghosts have always been a part of my life. Unlike most Mediums, and I am not a Medium, I do not believe encouraging communication with ghosts is a good thing. If a ghost becomes aware that you know they are near, or that you can or are willing to communicate with them, they will pester you until they can get their message across to you, and some ghosts can become a danger to you. So, I have finally learned to shut them out or, at least ignore them and not let them know that I know they are in the vicinity. They can be very annoying when they are trying to get your attention. A family member will move on if you wave and go about your business, but other apparitions will not.

It was the third house I remembered living in and it was full of ghosts. They mostly hung around the stairwell and the upstairs closet that ran between the two bedrooms. There was also a closet underneath the steps that took you upstairs. Access to the closet could be gained through a door from the living room. My sister and I never opened the door to the closet or played in it.

During the very cold winter months our only heat in the old house was a coal stove in the middle of the living room, so when my sister and I were very small, mom and dad would set up a bed for my us at the North end of the living room. The bed was directly in front of the door leading under the stairwell.

One night when I was 5 or 6 years old I woke up and there was a hand on my leg. I kept thinking how can that be because I was sleeping next to the wall, yet I touched the hand and felt the fingers. I knew I was awake and I pinched the hand and it didn't move and I didn't feel the pinch on my leg.

Mom and Dad were sleeping in the next room and I called out, "Mom!" No answer. "Mom!" No answer. After about four calls she finally said, "Shut up and go back to sleep." I said "There is a hand on my leg." When I said that, the hand disappeared. Mom said, "You are imagining things, go back to sleep."

I didn't think I was imagining anything and I quickly moved over to the middle of the bed closer to my sister.

In traditional belief and fiction, a ghost (sometimes known as a Spectre (British English) or specter (American English), phantom, apparition or spook) is the soul or spirit of a dead person or animal that can appear, in visible form or other manifestation, to the living. Descriptions of the apparition of ghosts vary widely from an invisible presence to translucent or barely visible wispy shapes, to realistic, lifelike visions. The deliberate attempt to contact the spirit of a deceased person is known as necromancy, or in Spiritism as a séance. http://en.wikipedia.org/wiki/Ghost

You could refer to a ghost as spirit beings. The Bible refers to spirit beings as angels and demons. 2 Corinthians 11-14-15 states: "14 And no marvel; for Satan himself is transformed into an angel of light. 15 Therefore, it is no great thing if his ministers also are transformed as the ministers of righteousness; whose end shall be according to their works." There are those that say since the devil masquerades as angels of light and servants of righteousness that appearing as a ghost and impersonating a deceased human would be within his power.

Ghosts or spirit beings were not unknown in biblical times. In Matthew where you read the story of the disciples on the ship when the storm came up in the St. James Version of the Bible at Matthew 14:26 "26 And when the disciples saw him walking on the sea, they were troubled, saying, 'It is a spirit; and they cried out for fear.'" The NIV Bible calls it a ghost rather than a spirit.

After Jesus was resurrected and appeared to his disciples they were afraid. He said to them, "Why are you troubled, and why do doubts rise in your minds? Look at my hands and my feet. It is I myself! Touch me and see; a ghost does not have flesh and bones, as you see I have." (Luke 24:37-39, NIV)

If you talk to a clergyman about ghosts, they will inform you that ghosts do not exist. Their analysis is that the Bible says when we die we immediately pass on to either heaven or hell. I believe the clergy do us all a great injustice by preaching that way. I guess they want to keep it simple.

Many people believe that ghosts are deceased people looking for vengeance or imprisoned on earth for bad things they did during life. The appearance of a ghost has often been regarded as an omen or portent of death. However, my father told me of a time when he was very ill and that some of his deceased family members stood at the foot of his bed and told him not to worry, that his time had not yet come.

Places where ghosts are reported to be found are described as haunted, and often seen as being inhabited by spirits of deceased who may have been former residents or were familiar with the property. Supernatural activity inside homes is said to be mainly associated with violent or tragic events in the building's past such as murder, accidental death, or suicide — sometimes in the recent or ancient past. I believe, in some cases, at least, a ghost will stay in a particular place until it can pass on a particular message and when that message can be delivered, the ghost can be liberated and move on.

For instance, the Hebrew Bible contains a few references to ghosts, associating Spiritism with forbidden occult activities cf. Deuteronomy 18:10-12 states: "10. There shall not be found among you any one that maketh his son or his daughter to pass through the fire, or that useth divination, or an observer of times, or an enchanter, or a witch. 11 Or a charmer, or a consulter with familiar spirits, or a wizard, or a necromancer. 12 For all that do these things are an abomination unto the Lord: and because of these abominations the Lord thy God doth drive them out from before thee."

What is 'familiar spirits' if not ghosts?

The most notable reference is in the First Book of Samuel. In 1 Samuel 11, Saul was worried about fighting with the Philistines and went to see the witch of Endor and asked her to call up Samuel from the grave. When the "ghostly" figure of an old man appeared, the witch of Endor was alarmed. Samuel told Saul he would lose the battle. (I Samuel 28:3–19 KJV), in which a disguised King Saul has the Witch of Endor summon the spirit/ghost of Samuel.

"3 Now Samuel was dead, and all Israel had lamented him, and buried him in Ramah, even in his city. And Saul had put away those that had familiar spirits, and the wizards, out of the land. 4 And the Philistines gathered themselves together and came and pitched in Shunem: and Saul gathered all Israel together, and they pitched in Gilboa. 5 And when Saul saw the host of the Philistines, he was afraid, and his heart greatly trembled. 6 And when Saul enquired of the Lord, the Lord answered him not, neither by dreams, nor by Urim, nor by prophets. 7 Then said Saul unto his servants, "Seek me a woman that hath a familiar spirit, that I may go to her, and enquire of her." And his servants said to him, "Behold, there is a woman that hath a familiar spirit at Endor." 8 And Saul disguised himself, and put on other raiment, and he went, and two men with him, and they came to the woman by night: and he said, 'I pray thee, divine unto me by the familiar spirit, and bring me him up, whom I shall name unto thee.' 9 And the woman said unto him, 'Behold, thou knowest what Saul hath done, how he hath cut off those that have familiar spirits, and the wizards, out of the land: wherefore then layest thou a snare for my life, to cause me to die?' 10 And Saul sware to her by the Lord, saying, 'As the Lord liveth, there shall no punishment happen to thee for this thing.' 11 Then said the woman, 'Whom shall I bring up unto thee?' And he said, 'Bring me up Samuel.' 12 And when the woman saw Samuel, she cried with a loud voice: and the woman spake to Saul, saying, 'Why hast thou deceived me? for thou art Saul.' 13 And the king said unto her, 'Be not afraid: for what sawest thou?' And the woman said unto Saul, 'I saw gods ascending out of the earth.' 14 And he said unto her, 'What form is he of?' And she said, 'An old man cometh up; and he is covered with a mantle.' And Saul perceived that it was Samuel, and he stooped with his face to the ground, and bowed himself. 15 And Samuel said to Saul, 'Why hast thou disquieted me, to bring me up?' And Saul answered, "I am sore distressed; for the Philistines make war against me, and God is departed from me, and answereth me no more, neither by prophets, nor by dreams: Therefore, I have called thee, that thou mayest make known unto me what I shall do." 16 Then said Samuel, "Wherefore then dost thou ask of me, seeing the Lord is departed from thee, and is become thine enemy? 17 And the Lord hath done to him, as he spake by me: for the Lord hath rent the kingdom out of thine hand, and given it to thy neighbour, even to David: 18 Because thou obeyedst not the voice of the Lord, nor executedst his fierce wrath upon Amalek, therefore hath the Lord done this thing unto thee this day. 19 Moreover the Lord will also deliver Israel with thee into the hand of the Philistines: and tomorrow shalt thou and thy sons be with me: The Lord also shall deliver the host of Israel into the hand of the Philistines."

There was widespread belief in ghosts in ancient Egyptian culture in the perspective of the continued existence of the soul and spirit after death, with the ability to assist or harm the living, and the possibility of a second death. Over a period of more than 2,500 years, Egyptian beliefs about the nature of the afterlife evolved constantly.

Egyptians have always believed that the soul continued to live after death. However, their beliefs in ghosts constantly changed throughout history. "Early ancient Egyptians thought that part of the human soul was made up of a separate entity not unlike other religions' beliefs in a god giving life to all people. This "other" part of man was described as "light" and called, "Khu." Later, the definition of Khu would morph into a word for ill-spirited ghosts that possess the bodies of the living for purposes of torment (sort of a more-scary meaning, similar to popular beliefs in demons, if you will).

'These ancient Egyptian beliefs in the soul and spirit would later become more complex and consist of 5 parts: the heart (thoughts and feelings), shadow (we can assume this to mean the darker or negative nature of man), soul (the personality known as "Ba"), spirit (the life-giving source known as "Ka") and name. When the body expires, the Ba and Ka were believed to be back together, again, and called the "Akh." It is the Akh that is said to be the spirits (or possibly ghosts) of Egyptian people. The Akh could be either a blessing or curse upon the living, effectively interacting with people to affect their feelings, both positively or negatively. Akh, Egyptian "ghosts," have been blamed for things such as bad dreams, ailments and mental suffering. This idea would be very similar to modern spiritual beliefs in "ghost attachments." http://www.angelsghosts.com/egyptian-ghosts

Although the Bible refers to a ghost as a necromancer, the definition of a necromancer is more commonly referred to as a deceased ancestor, or ghosts of your ancestors, or perhaps calling on a witch that casts a spell through various rituals such as black magic.

Another interesting form I am sure you have heard of is the Poltergeists. The name is derived from the German poltern (to knock) and geist (spirits) and is generally defined as mischievous and sometimes malevolent spirits which are typically featured by raps, bumps, thumps, knocks, footsteps, and bed shaking, all without an obvious point of origin. There are also many descriptions of reported objects being thrown about rooms, rains of dirt or other small objects, vile smells, furniture being moved or thrown about, and even people being levitated or assaulted. Historically, poltergeist activity has been attributed to the devil, demons, or witches; such activity has also been suggested to be an unconscious use of psychokinetic abilities. Although skeptics argue that all such phenomena can be explained through physical mechanisms or fraud, many continue to believe in spiritual or parapsychological causes.

Some of you may have watched the movie "Poltergeist" on television, or watched other creepy, or not so menacing ghost movies. Casper was the cute, friendly ghost. Watching a movie and living in a house where there are ghosts residing is a totally different experience. Perhaps if you are not sensitive to their presence, it would not bother you, but I have always been cognizant of when they are around. I have always had some extra-sensory abilities as far as knowing when the phone is going to ring and who is calling, when I am going to receive a letter from someone, or somebody is going to stop by the house or little things like that; but ghosts are a different legend, and I have never cared for their company. And if you visit a house that is truly haunted (having ghosts residing within), you do not need to have extra-sensory abilities. Ghosts have a way of letting you know they are present.

I was subjected to ghosts at a very early age. They were not something I sought out, but something that I thought everyone was aware of and what became a fairly common occurrence around our house.

There were creaking noises in the stairwell. I was about six or seven years old, my sister two years older.

"Did you hear that noise?"

"Yes, my sister responded.

"There it is again. Maybe if we turn the light on it will stop."

Honestly, my sister was about the bravest person I knew. I don't know how she does it. How can you know there are ghosts out there in the stairwell and still get out of bed, walk across the room to the open door next to the stairway where they are, and turn on the light switch?

I was hoping mom and dad didn't see our light through their windows. Their room is directly under ours. We were trying not to talk softly.

"Oh, you know there isn't anything out there," she said, yet she had admitted hearing the noises too.

"Yes, there is," I replied - perhaps too quickly. "If there weren't you wouldn't have fallen down the stairs and knocked yourself out a few weeks ago. I remember when you fell. Mom made me run to the kitchen to get a glass of water."

"Well, you know how steep and dark the stairs are, and I just tripped," she responded as she ran back to bed and crawled under the covers. "The steps were probably just creaking."

I knew better. She was following me down the stairs and we were both running down as usual.

It was such a cold night that the snow was coming between the glass and the window cross tees. It's too bad she didn't like me better, I thought as she kicked me for putting my cold feet on her legs.

"Well," I whispered, "what about when mom and dad are gone, and you don't want to come in the house?"

"Well you don't want to come in the house either. Everything is dark and spooky."

"He he," I giggled remembering she was the one that used the closet, not me. "You know at least one ghost hides in the closet between these two bedrooms, I reminded her."

"Well, why don't you sleep downstairs?"

"I don't have a bed downstairs."

"Well, I wish you did. I'm always getting in trouble for something you did." And there ain't no such thing as ghosts either."

"Yes, there is."

"No, there isn't. Go to sleep."

"Yes, there is," I said, always having to have the last word.

"You kids turn that light off," Mom yelled up.

"I'm not goin over there and turnin it off. There's ghosts over there," I murmured to my sister.

When I grew older, during the summer time I moved into the other upstairs bedroom. To some extent, it was because my sister wanted her own room, but I also found there was a nice breeze that would come through the West windows at night. I did, however, hate the fact that there was not a door on the closet that went between my room and my sister's room since I knew there was, at least, one ghost that stayed in there. I felt fairly safe at night if I kept the door to the stairway closed. During the winter, I moved my bed to a spare room downstairs.

When I graduated from high school, 18 years old, I left home and moved into a basement apartment in the city. I instinctively knew that near where the bed was someone had died a horrible death. I felt it when I rented the apartment, but I ignored the feeling. How many times in your life do you tell yourself that you should never ignore your gut instincts? It is one thing to deal with a situation like that in the daylight, but it is an entirely different thing to try to deal with it when you crawl into bed at night.

I was a court reporter working in the Coroner's Office, so I started going through some of the old files. Anyone stopping by the office would have found me covered with dust from head to toe, but I found what I was searching for. The first piece of paper in the file was a newspaper clipping headlined "Man Killed in Basement Apartment." After reading the newspaper account of how the man was stabbed, and scanning through the rest of the file, I put the file back in the filing cabinet. I figured I had enough and I marched outside of my office and picked up a newspaper at the kiosk and started skimming the rental ads for a new place to live.

As the years went by, my extra-sensory abilities seemed to intensify with no help from me. I had been working for several years on our family genealogy, and I guess Great Grandfather had decided that this gave him carte blanche to my personal territory since my search ended with him and I could not find out from where he came. I had a lovely antique wooden rocker in my bedroom, and when I wanted to take an afternoon nap on the weekend, the rocker would begin to rock. It was not a rocker that could rock by a slight breeze, or if jarred. It was a heavy, antique piece of furniture with big springs. I had always tried to ignore the rocking, but it was not only getting on my nerves, I felt I knew who it was, and he was infringing on my space. One day I got fed up, and I shook my finger at the chair and yelled, "Get out of my house and don't ever come back again." It worked. That rocker never rocked by itself again. Or was it Brother Evans?

Sometime around 1978, I got a divorce and bought a condominium. It was at that time that I ran into another ghost(s) – Lloyd and Georgie. I was excited about having my own place and getting on with my new life.

When I first moved into my new residence, I used the second bedroom as an office and would intermittently play games there on my new computer. When darkness started arriving, I would begin feeling uneasy about being in that room. It was nothing I could put my finger on, but there was something about the closet that bothered me. I never thought about it being a ghost. I remember looking in the closet and I didn't even have any clothes hanging in it. I had not been disturbed by real ghosts for quite a while, so I did not immediately consider that as a possibility. I would just have this dreadful uneasiness, so I would shut down the computer, leave the room and go to my bedroom to read or watch television.

At first, when I was laying in my bed reading, I would see flickers of light in my dresser mirror which was directly at the foot of the bed. "The lights must be from cars going by," I thought. "Wait a minute, there are no cars going by the house. If I look directly at the mirror, I didn't see anything. If I look at my book or elsewhere, I would see the flashes. What is going on?" Then I realized the flashes were coming from the hallway outside my bedroom door and I would see the reflection in my dresser mirror.

I read some place that is how you detect a ghost is near.

My condo was a two-story, two-bedroom and a bath upstairs and kitchen, dining area, living room, laundry, and half-bath downstairs.

During the summer time the upstairs was always hot even with the air conditioning so late at night I found that if I opened the patio door in my bedroom and the window in the guest bedroom there was a wonderful breeze that would go through the two bedrooms and cool off the upstairs rooms.

Many nights I would wake up with my back to the bedroom door and have this terrifying feel like someone was behind me and I would have to turn over because I would feel like someone was staring at me and about to touch me. But I kept telling myself I was imagining things.

Quite often if it was very late and I was still up reading, I would feel like someone entered my room and was watching me. At first I wasn't afraid. It was just an annoyance. It was always at the same hour of the night, 11:00, and it would last ten minutes or so. I could set my clock by it. I would look at my clock and it was always 11:00 p.m.

"I should have driven the back roads home from work," I thought. The expressway traffic is bumper to bumper and down to a crawl. I'm in the fast lane and somehow in the next quarter of a mile, I have to cross three lanes of traffic to get to my off ramp. I turned on my turn signal to make my move, and I eased my car over through the traffic and then headed down the ramp and down my street.

Cleaning house at 5:00 p.m. will almost be a welcome relief I reasoned as I pulled into my parking spot. I checked my mailbox, unlocked my door, and then headed straight up the stairs to my bedroom where I began changing clothes.

I picked up some ironing I had brought up that morning and took it to the other bedroom. I tossed it inside into a laundry basket and quickly closed the door. I headed down the stairs while thinking about what cleaning supplies I would need.

When I arrived downstairs, the radio was turned on in the kitchen. My senses perked up. I never turn on that radio. The only reason I have it is for the clock.

Over and over my mind was playing "it was not on this morning when I got up. It was not on this morning when I left for work. And it was not on when I came home from work or I would have heard it when

I came in the front door." It was not on because I never turn on that radio. I checked both doors and no one had broken in.

I tried to ignore the obvious. I had not had this feeling for many years. I reached over and turned the radio off, collected my cleaning supplies, and proceeded back up the stairs.

When I reached the top of the stairs, the door to the spare bedroom was wide open. I tried to tell myself that maybe I had not closed it tight enough and it eased open. But even if that were true the door would only be ajar and not completely wide open. I was surprised, yet irritated. I reached over and closed the door again. I do not like uninvited intruders.

I went into my room with the hopes of forgetting about it. I laid my cleaning supplies on the bed and walked over to my dressing table and saw that the items there were in disarray. My hand mirror was turned upside down, and the perfume bottles were knocked over. Someone or something was trying to get my attention, and I did not intend to acknowledge it.

Apparently, this ghost had become aware that I knew of its presence in my home and was now attempting to communicate or get my complete attention. He had it.

A couple of days later, I went out with a girlfriend to play Bingo.

"Aileen, I need to tell you something, but I don't want you to think I'm crazy."

"Oh, come on, I know you better than that. Tell me," she said.

"I think I have a ghost at my house."

She, of course, could not contain herself. She burst out laughing at me. "You're kidding?"

"I'm serious. Every night at 11:00 p.m., or 10:00 depending on the time change, if I have the door open to the spare bedroom, this ghost comes out in the hallway and stands at the door of my bedroom. Sometimes he will step just inside the door so that he can see me. He stands there for about 10 minutes."

"Let's go talk to him," she said. She is always game for new adventures.

"You're out of your mind," I told her.

"No, I want to see if I can feel him being there."

She had told me on other occasions about some of her psychic experiences, so I thought about it for a few minutes. I knew it could be dangerous, but I had never felt fear from this particular ghost, only uneasiness, so I finally said, "Okay, he doesn't come out until 11:00 p.m. and Bingo is over at 10:00, so that gives us plenty of time." Frankly, I wanted confirmation that it was not just me.

We drove back to my house, and we went straight upstairs. I opened the door to the guest bedroom. By then I was making it a habit of keeping that door closed. I found my tape recorder, and I set it up. I turned the clock so that I could see it and I sat Aileen on the bed so that her back was to the door and the clock. We just sat there on the bed chatting.

At 11:00 P.M. I could feel it, but I was careful not to look at the door or at the clock. Aileen bristled, and the hairs stood up on both our arms and she said, "Oh, my gosh!" She paused and then said, "I feel like there is a man and a small child." She never did turn around.

I said, "So that's why I never felt any fear. I never sensed the child."

All of a sudden, I felt compelled to write. I had been involved with automatic writing on one previous occasion. I found some paper and a pencil in my nightstand on the opposite side from the door and it was not long before my hand began to move. I ended up writing "Lloyd I'm sorry I ran I couldn't help." In about 10 minutes, it was all over.

Aileen and I attempted to play the tape back and at first, there was nothing at all on the tape. My friend angrily said, "Now listen, I know at least our voices should be on the tape." We played it back again, and our voices were on the tape, and then there was silence, and then there was this child's voice on the tape in a singing, eerie voice that said "Georgie Cookie."

Matters got worse after that. I had a dream that night that Lloyd was in the backseat of Aileen's car as she drove home. Aileen called me the next morning and said she thought Lloyd was in the backseat of her car when she drove home.

After that, I had several attempts of possession where Lloyd was attempting to get into my body while I was sleeping and the only way I could avoid this from happening was to scream and put forth enough of my own energy to keep him out. When I would wake up, it would be

11:00 p.m. I would also have other nights where I would wake up with this very strong feeling someone was directly behind me and about to touch me. I would turn over and look at the clock, and it would always be 11:00 p.m. You know that feeling you get when you know someone is staring at you, and you look up, and they are? Multiply that feeling by about one hundred fifty, or maybe more, and if it is someone really ugly and menacing you will understand my meaning. If it wakes you up from a sound sleep, you know it is really strong.

Finally, I put my Condominium up for sale and moved. But Lloyd wanted contact again. I supposed because he knew that I knew he was around. He moved with me. I bought a four-bedroom house, and he moved into the bedroom that had the attic access. I didn't realize that until I would go into that particular bedroom and go into the walk-in closet with the attic door. There would be insulation on the floor and I had not opened the attic door. So I started keeping the door to that closet and the door to the bedroom closed and yet when I would go past that room, the door would shake like someone had a hold of the door knob and was shaking the door. Of course, I took off in the other direction. The episode with what I thought was Lloyd lasted a few months, and then it stopped. I assume Lloyd moved on and I almost forgot about him. I still kept that room off limits unless I had company.

Ghosts are very capable and willing to communicate with living people. Communicating with ghosts is not a new idea. Every religion in the world has views on the subject. Communicating with the dead is one of mankinds' oldest beliefs. It has only been in the last hundred years or so that people have begun to deny ghosts and spirits.

Free will exists beyond the physical body. Sometimes a spirit chooses not to go to the light. Sometimes an addiction will cause a person not to go to the light because they are more focused on their need than the light.

Talking to ghosts has become big business, and professional psychics charge large fees. Believers hold that there are several ways of communicating with the dead if the belief and the willpower are there.

The Ouija Board has a bad reputation but is one way of communicating with the dead for those who are not easily spooked and is relatively harmless. It can also be great fun for the party crowd. It has been around since 1890 and was originally used as a toy. It wasn't until World War One when an American spiritualist called Pearl Curran used an Ouija board as a divining tool that it became just that.

I personally believe a Ouija Board can be used for good or evil. While my father was still alive, we made a pact that whoever died first would attempt to make contact with the person that is alive as proof of life after death. Perhaps some people would be anxious to have contact with their lost loved ones, and as close as I was to my father, I kept closed up and did not want contact.

It was several years after his death when a friend and I pulled out a Ouija Board and my father immediately came through on it. I had been struggling with a question in my life and with one word my father answered that question. I did not even ask the question. He confirmed at the beginning who he was, and we asked if he had a message and he left me a one-word message that only I would understand. It was like touching a hot stove. Maybe others would have handled the situation differently, but I immediately put the Board away and have never touched it since. I do not even know if I still have the Ouija Board any place in my home, or if I threw the Board away.

Frankly, I do not know why my father and I made that pact. I have always believed that when someone passes to the next dimension that they are on God's time and it is something you must accept. Someday I will also be there. Everyone handles a loved one's passing differently. Yes, it leaves a hole in your chest for quite a long while. And it hurts. But you have to releases them to God and the sooner you do, the sooner your pain will ease. The person that passed sees your pain and wishes you did not experience it. The person that passed has no more pain and feels only love.

Automatic writing is a form of spirit communication where any writing produced is said to come from spirits and not the writer. Having first appeared in the early 1900s, automatic writing has become a small but valuable niche in spiritualist and medium movements ever since. Nowadays it is practiced under its more scientific name of psychography. I have had two experiences of automatic writing in my lifetime. Once with Lloyd as described above and one time when my spirit guide needed to contact me to reassure me that I would be okay in a situation where I had contemplated taking my own life. That was one of the most comforting moments of my life.

I came from a very religious family. No one had ever gotten a divorce. I was married to a sleaze that disrespected me from the first week of our marriage by his infidelity. For seventeen years, I acted like it was not happening and was the good wife my religion said I should be. For the last two years, I cried every day because I was so unhappy and I felt I could not get a divorce. I figured the only other choice I had was to run away or to kill myself. I was not thinking about any pain I would cause others or inflict upon myself. I did not think about where I would spend eternity. I just knew I could not go on in this marriage. As I sat on the side of the bed with a gun in my hand contemplating ending my life, it was then that I heard a voice - out loud – in my bedroom – behind me – and it said, "God will not forgive you." With all my heart, I believe that voice was the voice of my spirit guide.

It was shortly after that when I was sitting at my desk in my office when I had my first experience with automatic writing. I was caught up on all my work, and I was sitting there with a pen in my hand staring out the window. I was always ready to go into my boss' office to take dictation, so my hand was next to a steno pad. I don't recall that I was thinking of anything in particular. I just remember watching the construction crew building the hotel across the street. All of a sudden, my hand started moving on the notebook.

I had read about automatic writing but had never experienced it and did not know exactly how it worked. I was surprised about what was occurring, but I felt I knew what was happening and I just relaxed and continued to stare out the window and tried not to think about my hand moving on the pad. Once in a while, I find the message in a drawer some place here at home, and then I lose it again or forget where it is. The general message was "we know you will do what is best for you and that you will be okay." At the time, I had no idea what I was writing. I was not thinking these words or anything similar while this was happening. I don't even know if I was thinking about my problems at the time. And it definitely was not my handwriting. There was construction work on a new hotel going on across the street from my office, and I tried to concentrate on the construction crew as opposed to what was happening with my hand. With automatic writing, there are no spaces between words. All the letters run together as one long word so that it comes out as "weknowyouwilldowhatisbestforyouandthatyouwillbeokay."

I somehow felt comforted by the message, although at the time I wondered who it came from. In those days we did not have the internet and I had not read much about angels and spirit guides, but even now though I do not know who the writer of the message was, I believe the "we" he was referring to was my angels and spirit guides and that the message had to have come from my spirit guides.

Most practitioners of psychography believe they are making direct contact with benevolent spirits. I personally believe it is a dark occult as is the Ouija Board and that any time you invite an unknown spirit to take over a part of your body, you are inviting extreme danger and harm to come to you. I do believe that is why the Bible warns you not to engage in any way, shape, or form with any occult activity whatsoever. You cannot control what a spirit will do to you.

As to my first experience, I do not believe I was in any danger as I am confident this was my spirit guide. But in the second instance, I was inviting danger, because I did not know Lloyd, or whoever was attempting to contact Lloyd. I can only imagine that a man and a little girl were killed, or in an accident outside of my house, and this man was carrying around such guilt that he could not move on, and he needed to apologize to Lloyd because he could not help him. But as it turned out this spirit wanted more contact and became more violent. Or perhaps he was not a human ghost, but a demon parading as a human ghost. Or, perhaps he was frustrated that I could not deliver the message to Lloyd. Either way he seemed unable to move on and I did not have the experience to help him.

Psychography and Ouija Boards can be said to be connected since they both use the same sort of technique. Both of these methods rely on a spirit taking over the hand of whoever is trying to communicate with them. This can lead to either very good results or complete gibberish depending, it is believed, on the skill of the person attempting it. I believe it is on the skill of the person attempting to give you a message. If you are getting gibberish, ask your spirit to start over slowly, and your message will come through. It is necessary in either instance that you ask if it is a good spirit. If it responds that it is, you can proceed. If it does not respond, do not proceed.

And, there is, of course, EVP, or electronic voice phenomena, and Séances that became popular with the rise of spiritualism. http://scribol.com/anthropology-and-history/spirit-communication-how-do-mediums-speak-with-the-dead

There is nothing so curious as a Séance. Some Mediums offer comfort and mystery. Then you have the fake and fraudsters who exploit the vulnerable. We have been attempting to commune with the dead since ancient times. God finally told us in Leviticus not to have anything to do with Mediums.

It is my belief that if the Lost Scriptures were included in the Bible, then mankind would believe that when you die your body goes to another dimension until Judgment Day. No one can otherwise explain how Mediums can communicate with the dead or how just plain ole people like me can communicate with a ghost or sense when a ghost is around.

I now live in a brand-new house that I had built from the ground up. I thought that way I would never have to be thinking about ghosts. But it does not work that way. You have relatives that pass on and they want to visit with you and see if you are okay. I do not know why they hang around. There is that old expression "your mom or your dad or your husband, etc. is watching over you." Well, it is true. I have double doors that lead to my bedroom, and just outside of those two doors I get two visitors that usually stop by together; a cousin, Lea, and my father. Now and then I will just wave in the direction of the doors to let them know that I am aware of their presence, and then I go back to watching television or working on my computer.

Last June I lost my best friend, a Pomeranian named Sashy. We were inseparable. We were very close and could read each other's minds. She visits me quite often. I still feel her jump up on the bed at night and walk around. Sometimes I catch a glimpse or flash of her in the room if I have moved my head fast. Now I have a new Pom and it is like she knows when Sash is around and she stays away from the end of the bed where Sash used to lay.

The fact that there are ghosts communicating with live people, at least, to me, is proof of life after death, or that we never really die.

Do I believe there is life after death, or that life continues? Absolutely. And after you have finished reading this book, I hope that I will have convinced you that life does not end when your physical bodies returns to dust.

Banshees

The banshee is a female spirit in Irish mythology, usually seen as an omen of death and a messenger from another world. Legend has it that a banshee is a fairy woman who begins to wail if someone is about to die. There have been alleged sightings of banshees as late as 1948.

Banshees are an Irish myth and attach to Irish families. Most surnames attached to banshees have the O or Mc/Mac prefix, or last names Power or Oswald. It is said that a banshee's cry predicts the death of a member of one of Ireland's five major families: The O'Grady's, the O'Neills, the O'Briens, the O'Connors or the Kavanaghs. A banshee's first name commonly begins with a C or K, such as C/Kleo or C/Kiara, which indicates their name is native to Ireland. This also indicates that their name is associated with the Airlie clan. Records of banshees go back as far as 1380 when Sean mac Craith published *Triumphs of Torlough*. Other accounts of banshees were found in Norman literature of that time.

Although a banshee is often described as stunningly beautiful, a fairy, and as being dressed in a white or gray dress with long pale hair which they comb with a silver comb. They have also been described as being dressed in green, red, or black with a gray cloak, and some have described them most often as an ugly, frightening hag.

The banshee may also appear in a variety of other forms, such as that of a hooded crow, stoat, hare, and weasel – animals associated in Ireland with witchcraft. Some say her keening can be so piercing that it would break glass, a low, pleasant singing, the sound of two boards being stuck together, a thin, screeching sound somewhere between the wail of a woman and the moan of an owl, all depending on what part of the country you are from.

There are stories of banshees in North Carolina and South Dakota in the Eighteenth Century. https://en.wikipedia.org/wiki/Banshee

IV

SPIRITUALISM

The term "Spiritualism" is a monotheistic belief system or religion, proposing a belief in one God, but with the distinct belief that spirits of the dead residing in the spirit world can be contacted by "mediums," who can then provide information about the afterlife.

In contrast, "Spiritism," the religion, prospered for a half century without legendary texts or formal organization, achieving unity by publications, tours by trance lecturers, and missionary activities of accomplished mediums. Several of the renowned Spiritualists were women. Most of the disciples supported other causes such as the abolition of slavery and women's suffrage. By the late 1880s, the credibility of the informal movement had weakened due to accusations of fraud among mediums and formal Spiritualist organizations began to appear.

Spiritualism, the religion, is currently practiced primarily through various denominational Spiritualist Churches in the United States and the United Kingdom.

Spiritism has supporters in many countries throughout the world, including Spain, United States, Canada, Japan, Germany, France, England, Argentina, Portugal and especially Brazil, which has the largest proportion and greatest number of followers.

The Spiritualist movement was an American invention. Although the idea that man could communicate with spirits has existed for centuries, modern belief came about in 1848 in New York when two sisters named Margaret and Kate Fox decided to communicate with a peddler that was murdered in a Hydesville house after attempting to sell his wares to Mrs. Bell.

Legend has it that a woman named Lucretia Pulver acted as a maid, cook and cleaning lady at the Bell household, and a young peddler came calling with his case of pots and pans and kitchen knives. It was suggested that he was very friendly, and he and Ms. Pulver enjoyed a perhaps closer than proper relationship that afternoon and Ms. Pulver was discharged from her duties.

Less than a week later, Ms. Pulver's services were again requested by Mrs. Bell, and although the Peddler was never seen again, several of his wares were seen at the kitchen of Mrs. Bell.

Shortly after that, Ms. Pulver began to notice strange noises about the house. There were tapping and footsteps. She also fell in a freshly turned patch of dirt in the cellar.

Soon after that, the Bells moved out, and the Weakmans moved in with a relative, Mrs. Lafe. Mrs. Lafe saw the apparition of a man in a black coat in the kitchen and when she screamed the man disappeared. They would hear rappings and footsteps during the daylight hours and at night, so they abandoned the house.

In 1848, the Fox Family moved into the house, and they had two young daughters, Margaret, and Kate. The banging and rattling began again. Kate woke up saying a cold hand touched her face. Margaret said someone pulled the covers off her bed. The mother said she heard footsteps going down into the cellar. Mr. Fox tried to find an explanation but could not.

On March 31, 1848, as Mr. Fox was going about knocking on walls trying to investigate the source of the problem, Kate noticed the rappings in return were the same number of knocks as if something was attempting to communicate with them.

Kate and her sister had nicknamed the presence "splitfoot." She called out and said, "do as I do!" She clapped her hands together two times. A few seconds later two knocks came from inside the walls. She rapped on the table, and the precise number of knocks came back from the presence.

A former tenant, William Duesler, was invited over, and he invented a series of knocks to create a form of the alphabet and a form of "yes" and "no" so he could communicate with the presence. Mr. Duesler was a former occupant of the house. He asked repeated questions and found out that the presence was the peddler who had been murdered and robbed years before. One of the neighbors present was the former maid, Mrs. Pulver, and she told of finding the loose dirt in the cellar. John Fox and William Duesler went to the cellar and began to dig, but all they found were some scraps of cloth and what looked like a piece of skull with some hair attached.

In 1904, a group of children was playing in the ruins of the home when the East wall of the home collapsed. A man that ran to the aid of the children said the reason for the collapse was it had a false partition poorly constructed in the past. Between the false brick wall and the genuine wall of the cellar were the bones of a man and a large box just like the one carried by the peddlers a few decades earlier. A portion of the man's skull was missing.

The two sisters went about the United States giving demonstrations of their so-called ability to communicate with spirits from the other side.

The Spiritualists believe that the dead can communicate through what are called "mediums." Mediums are sensitive persons who are in touch with another dimension, and they can pass along messages from the other side. Spiritualism was never meant to turn into a faith or religious movement. It was a popular past time and an amusing way to spend a long winter evening.

As well, the downfall of many of the mediums came about when many were exposed as fakes when they began swindling their naïve clients to line their pockets. That is not to say that all spiritualists were dishonest.

Some very notable spiritualists are:

Judge John W. Edmonds (1816 - 1874) was one of the most influential early American Spiritualists. After a great public career, as a member of both branches of the New York State Legislature and, for some time, President of the Senate and Judge of the Supreme Court of New York, he resigned the latter position on account of the outcry raised against his Spiritualistic beliefs and, especially, his support of the Fox sisters.

1918 Sir Arthur Conan Doyle (1858 - 1930) proclaimed his belief in the teachings and truth of Spiritualism. Just as Andrew Jackson Davis was called the 'John the Baptist' of Modern Spiritualism, Sir Arthur Conan Doyle was called the 'St. Paul' of Spiritualism. He was a prolific writer on the subject and an avid proponent. 1920 The famous British crusader, Sir Arthur Conan Doyle, paid a visit to New Zealand which aroused great interest. While here, he made visits to a number of centres and gave lectures which created both stimulus and direction to the Spiritualist movement.

Sir William F. Barrett (1845 - 1926) published his book 'On the threshold of the unseen; an examination of the phenomena of Spiritualism and of the evidence for survival after death'. Barrett made searching inquiries both in England and in the USA. His summing up was that there is evidence for the existence of a spirit world, for survival after death, and for occasional communication with those passed over.

1995 For many years that the Roman Catholic Church has been carrying out scientific experiments with their own mediums and one of the most competent theologians of the Vatican, Father Gino Concetti, writing in the 'Osservatore Romano', the daily paper of the Holy See, says that, 'According to the modern catechism the Church has decided not to forbid anymore to dialogue with the deceased ... this is as a sequel of new discoveries within the domain of the paranormal.'

1998 John Edwards was born and raised on Long Island, NY, exhibited psychic abilities from an extremely early age and was deemed 'special' by many in his family. The fact that he would uncannily know family history and events that took place before his birth solidified that fact. Because no fuss was made over these early experiences, he maintained as normal a childhood as possible. Since psychic phenomena were so accepted by his family, it was easy for his abilities to flourish.

In the 1840's, Allan Kardec, in France, claimed to be in contact with "The Spirit of Truth." He called it Spiritism and said it was for people that were spiritual but were "turned off" by organized religion; people who still believe in God and want to know how to live their lives according to His Will.

Kardec produced five books of Revelation which form the basis of Spiritism. Spiritists believe that these five books form the basis for their beliefs.

"Heaven and Hell" is divided into two parts and states that Heaven (happiness in the afterlife) and Hell (punishment in the afterlife) are misconceptions, that the state of the spirits after their death is not definitive and that there is always hope. The second part is a series of interviews with spirits of deceased people.

"The Genesis:" Miracles and Predictions Explained by the Spiritist Doctrine. This book attempts to find common ground between science and religion and dispel the supernatural.

"The Spirits' Book" presented a collection of FAQS by a respected and experienced educator who became a sensation overnight. Kardec concepts presented in the book were as follows:

"God is the supreme intelligence and primary cause of all things. God is eternal, immutable, unique, omnipotent, supremely just and good.

'The Universe is a creation of God. It encompasses all beings, whether they be rational or irrational, animate or inanimate, material or immaterial.

'Beyond the physical world, which is the habitation of incarnate Spirits (Mankind), there exists the spiritual world which is the habitation of discarnate Spirits.

'All the Laws of Nature are divine laws because God is their author. These Laws cover both the laws of physics and the moral laws.

'Man is an incarnate Spirit in a material body. The perispirit is a semi-material body which unites the Spirit to the material body.

'Spirits are the intelligent Beings of creation. They constitute the World of the Spirits, which pre-exists and survives everything.

'All Spirits are created simple and ignorant. They gradually evolve intellectually and morally, so passing from an inferior order to more elevated levels, till they finally reach perfection where they will enjoy constant happiness.

'All Spirits preserve their individuality, before, during and after each incarnation.

'Spirits reincarnate as many times as becomes necessary in order to achieve their own perfection.

'The different corporeal existences of the Spirit are always progressive and never regressive. The rapidity of their progress, both intellectually and morally, depends upon the degree of effort made towards betterment.

'Jesus is the guide and model for all Humanity. The Doctrine which he taught and exemplified is the most pure expression of God's Laws.

'The ethics of Jesus (excluding the religious dogmatic elements), contained in the Gospels, is a templete towards progress for all mankind, and its practice is the solution for all human problems.

'Man has free-will so as to act, but must respond for the consequences of his actions.

'The future life reserves penalties or compensations compatible and in accordance with Man's behavior while incarnate, as to whether or not God's Laws were respected.

'Prayer is an act of adoration towards God. It is contained within Natural Law, being the result of an innate sentiment of Man, just as the idea of the existence of a Creator is also innate in Man.

'Prayer helps Man to become better. Those who pray with fervor and confidence find themselves to be stronger against the temptations of ignorant forces, and God sends them Good Spirits to assist them. This is help that is never denied to those who ask with true sincerity."

"The Mediums Book," also written by Allan Kardec, contains the theoretic explanation of the diverse phenomena and of the conditions of mediumship in which they are produced. But the section pertaining to the development and exercise of mediumship was a topic of particular attention and focus."

"The Gospel According to Spiritualism," by Allan Kardec. It is said, "The core message this book presents transcends time and religious form, as Allan Kardec carefully chose passages from the Gospel that deal exclusively with moral matters and timeless truths. In doing so, he deliberately avoided what might be interpreted as circumstantial to the Jewish nation and customers. These scripture excerpts became the basis for the explanations provided by the Spirits, and the explications by Allan Kardec, himself." http://www.sgny.org/spiritism-guide/the-5-book-codification-ii/

Surprisingly enough, most people that do not attend church or temple, or an organized religious group, still believe in God or a higher power and pray to that power daily. As do the spiritualists, most of mankind believes that prayer helps Man to become better. They believe in Jesus Christ and some even read the Bible. You cannot knock the ones that do not because many Christians that go to church do not read the Bible saying, "I do not understand what I am reading."

For those that do go to Church every Sunday and consider themselves to be "religious," I do hope you do not judge the people that pray every day to a higher power. I used to be what I considered a spiritualist. If I had not found spiritualism and prayed every day to a higher power, I would not have found my way back to God. In spiritualism, I discovered a loving God that I never found in the religion that I grew up learning about.

Some Spiritualisms believe in reincarnation, and organized religion does not, although there are some indications in the Bible that perhaps it could be true.

Interestingly, about 2% of the world is atheist and about 16% are just non-religious. Hopefully, that means the rest of the world believes in God or a higher power, or life after death.

A point often overlooked in religions are our attempts to worship and understand God. However, some religions limit God, who is limitless. Our purpose in our physical body is to become one with God. There are many religions because it is our nature to adapt truth to our particular positions.

It is important to realize that to believe in God is to believe in life after death.

I read where one man said he died and went to heaven. He asked God which religion was the true religion? God said, "I don't care." I like that. Doesn't that sound like something God would say?

I spent eighteen years being brought up learning the morals, beliefs, principles, tenets, codes and values of religion. They were pounded into me. What was missing? God's love. It was not until I was introduced to spiritualism through a twelve-step program that I learned the difference about how religion looks at God's love and how spiritualism looks at God's Love. I was brought up more in an atmosphere of "hell's fire and damnation" rather than love. If you sin you are going straight to hell. Well, I figured God couldn't possibly love me because I was always getting yelled at for something bad that I did. I could not possibly get into heaven because I was such an evil person. And I knew I could never be that good either. I was just a perpetual sinner. I spent my entire life feeling guilty about everything I did because it was never good enough. I would never measure up to my parents' expectations, so how could I ever measure up to God.

Spiritualism taught me that not only did God love me, but it taught me to love myself and to love God and others. It also eventually brought me back to religion so that I could worship God properly. I do not have to agree with everything the church stands for, but it is a place of worship and the purpose for going to church is to worship God.

How many times have you heard people complain when they go to church that they don't like this or they don't like that about the church? That means they are not going to church to worship God. They are going to church for the wrong reason. It may be that they are going to the wrong church, that they have not found the church that suits them, but they are still are not going to church to worship God. There still is a difference.

"Worship is giving God the best that He has given you. Be careful what you do with the best you have. Whenever you get a blessing from God, give it back to Him as a love-gift. Take time to meditate before God and offering the blessing back to Him in a deliberate act of worship. If you hoard it for yourself, it will turn into spiritual dry rot, as the manna did when it was hoarded (see Exodus 16:20). God will never allow you to keep a spiritual blessing completely for yourself. It must be given back to Him so that He can make it a blessing to others." http://utmost. org/worship/

I have never heard that used in a sermon before. I hear people say they are blessed and I have even made the statement that I am blessed. But I admit I am so selfish I have never thought about offering a blessing back to God so he can give it to someone else. When I think of how many blessings I receive that I just take for granted and you look around and see others that surely could use a few, I believe I will make it a point in my prayers to ask God to give some of my blessings to others.

V

REINCARNATION, PAST LIFE REGRESSION

Reincarnation is the belief that the human soul never perishes or dies; it simply passes through a succession of lives. In its basic concept, it had its origin in India sometime near 800 B.C. Reincarnation is vital to classical Buddhism and Hinduism.

The concept of karma is closely associated with reincarnation. Karma is essentially the law of cause and effect. Those that profess belief in karma teach that the deeds (good or bad) of one's past lives affect this present life. Further, ones' present deeds will have ramifications for future lives.

In other words, the law of sowing and reaping is not limited to this present life but rather continues throughout eternity. What it comes down to is how many times will you return, in what form, and where you will reincarnate? Also, how many times will you reincarnate?

The Hindu-Buddhist philosophy on reincarnation is that "good" life results in rebirth to a higher quality form, and "bad" life results in rebirth to a lower quality form of rebirth. This forward/backward progression is based on the law of Karma. We all know that Karma is a system where good deeds are rewarded, and bad deeds are punished. The ultimate goal is for the soul to progress to the highest level of existence and become one with the universe.

The Bible also contradicts the belief in karma by emphasizing grace. According to the Bible, atonement and forgiveness may be gained only through the death and bodily resurrection of Jesus Christ. Salvation is based solely upon the work of Jesus Christ, not upon our own merits. The concepts of reincarnation and karma are in clear contrast to Hebrews 9:27,

"For it is appointed for men to die once and after this comes judgment."

The Bible teaches that at death, while man's body is mortal, decays and returns to dust, his soul and spirit continue on, either in a place of torments (hell) for those who reject Christ or in paradise (heaven) in God's presence for those who have trusted in the Savior. Both categories of people will be resurrected, one to eternal judgment and the other to eternal life with a glorified body (John 5:24-30). The emphatic statement of the Bible, as will be pointed out below, is that "it is appointed unto men once to die and after that the judgment" (Heb. 9:27).

The one passage that some point to as evidence for reincarnation is Matthew 17:10-12 which links John the Baptist with Elijah. However, the passage does not say that John the Baptist was Elijah reincarnated but that he would have fulfilled the prophecy of Elijah's coming if the people had believed his words and thereby believed in Jesus as the Messiah (Matthew 17:12). The people specifically asked John the Baptist if he was Elijah, and he said, "No, I am not" (John 1:21). http://www.gotquestions.org/reincarnation.html#ixzz3MHDEPAwq

People that believe in reincarnation, however, believe that John the Baptist was Elijah because Luke 1:17 said that John the Baptist would precede Christ "with the spirit and power of Elijah." A reincarnation believer also refers to 2 Kings 2:11 where it says that Elijah never experienced physical death, and again in Matthew 17:3 when Elijah appeared with Moses at the Mount of Transfiguration. In John 3:3 Jesus tells Nicodemus that to see the Kingdom of God you must be born again. Reincarnationists believe that means that Jesus is talking about actual rebirth to achieve the cycle of perfection. Of course, Jesus set Nicodemus straight about an actual physical rebirth.

There are many Bible verses that would indicate that there is no such thing as reincarnation. For instance:

"Hebrews 9:27 - And as it is appointed unto men once to die, but after this the judgment.

'2 Corinthians 5:8 - We are confident, [I say], and willing rather to be absent from the body, and to be present with the Lord.

'Matthew 25:46 - And these shall go away into everlasting punishment: but the righteous into life eternal.

'Ecclesiastes 12:7 - Then shall the dust return to the earth as it was: and the spirit shall return unto God who gave it.

'Luke 23:43 - And Jesus said unto him, Verily I say unto thee, Today shalt thou be with me in paradise."

These are only a very few of the numerous verses recorded in the Bible. People that believe in reincarnation believe that we come back to a new life in a new body, and we can then atone for our past transgressions. Religions believe that you atone for your past transgressions and ask Jesus to forgive you of your transgressions while you are still in this physical body.

Although the majority of sects within the Abrahamic religions of Judaism, Christianity, and Islam do not believe that individuals reincarnate, particular groups within these religions do refer to reincarnation; these groups include the mainstream historical and contemporary followers of Kabbalah, the Cathars, the Druze and the Rosicrucians

Early Greek discussions on reincarnation have been found as early as the 6th Century BCE. Plato (428/427–348/347 BCE) presented accounts of reincarnation in his works, particularly the Myth of Er. However, authorities do not agree on how the idea arose in Greece.

Most compelling, we have "Psychiatrist Ian Stevenson, from the University of Virginia, who investigated many reports of young children who claimed to remember a past life. He conducted more than 2,500 case studies over a period of 40 years and published twelve books, including Twenty Cases Suggestive of Reincarnation and "*Where Reincarnation and Biology Intersect.*" Stevenson methodically documented each child's statements and then identified the deceased person the child identified with and verified the facts of the deceased person's life that matched the child's memory. He also matched birthmarks and birth defects to wounds and scars on the deceased, verified by medical records such as autopsy photographs, in *Reincarnation and Biology.*" http://en.wikipedia.org/wiki/Reincarnation.

Skeptic Carl Sagan asked the Dalai Lama what he would do if a fundamental tenet of his religion (reincarnation) were definitively disproved by science. The Dalai Lama answered, "If science can disprove reincarnation, Tibetan Buddhism would abandon reincarnation... but it's going to be mighty hard to disprove reincarnation."

In conjunction with this, past life regression is a technique that uses hypnosis to recover what practitioners believe are memories of past lives or incarnations, though others regard them as fantasies, or delusions, or a type of confabulation. Past life regression is typically undertaken either in pursuit of a spiritual experience or in a psychotherapeutic setting. Most advocates loosely adhere to beliefs about reincarnation, though religious traditions that incorporate reincarnation generally do not include the idea of repressed memories of past lives. http://en.wikipedia.org/wiki/Past_life_regression

Past life regression therapy has been progressed since the 1950s by psychologists, psychiatrists, and mediums. Practitioners believe that unresolved issues from alleged past lives may be the cause of their patients' problems. The Scientific consensus is that the memories are the result of cryptomnesia, narratives created by the subconscious mind using imagination, forgotten information and suggestions from the therapist. These memories can be more vivid than factual memories.

How many times have you heard someone say "we're soul mates?" Or how many times have you visited a place and experienced déjà vu?

Or how many times have you been introduced to someone and felt so at ease with them that you felt like you have known them all your life? Did any of these events make you think perhaps you had lived in a previous life? You can have more than one soul mate. I have gone into a store, for instance, and even though I am absolutely positive I have never been in that store, or that city before, and it is not a type of store I would ordinarily visit, and I would get sick to my stomach and swear that I had been there previously. I have friends today that I feel I have known for eternity.

Another key point for those that believe in reincarnation, it is said that you carry forward experiences, attitudes, and relationship dynamics from prior lives into our current lifetime. Sometimes that is beneficial if you have a skill in certain areas. Other times, traumatic experiences are left unresolved or troubled relationships are left in a state of conflict.

In regressive therapy, you re-experiencing the key events of a past-life and reprocessing the impact helps to bring closure to the events of that lifetime, which enables you to move forward more freely in the present.

Years ago, I read a book by Jess Stearn called "In Search of Taylor Caldwell." Ms. Caldwell is a well-known author who is also believed to have found the numinous entity while writing, for when she writes she uses phrases and words a layman would never know or use. She also does not believe in reincarnation but agreed to be hypnotized. Several sessions were involved, and each session was recorded. Ms. Caldwell was regressed into what were believed to be several past lives. After hearing her voice on the tapes and reliving many supposed past lives, Ms. Caldwell was invited to write the last chapter of the book. She still responded by saying she did not believe in reincarnation. Was she really in contact with her past lives, or other spirits?

I had a past-lives reading done locally as a lark. I never did meet the lady that gave the reading as it was done through the mail. The only thing that was asked of me was to write down the first names of ten people that I felt I had a connection with. I reasoned that I was doing this for fun, and I laughed the first time I read the report, but as I thought about it for about an hour later, it was not so funny.

There were too many "coincidences" in the reading. This lady gave me information about the people and gave me the actual names of other people presently in my life, which she should have no way of knowing. She also told me I had studied under a particular artist in a past life and said I could take up painting in this life if I chose. I do oil paint on occasion, and I do the same type of still life painting that this other artist did. She had no way of knowing that. I did not know that until I researched this other artist. Coincidence?

Do I believe in reincarnation? I do not know. Probably not because of my religious beliefs and what the Bible says.

Surprisingly, the belief in reincarnation is particularly high in the Baltic countries. Forty-four percent of Lithuanians believe in reincarnation. East Germany is the lowest at twelve percent. About one-third of the population of Russia believes in reincarnation. A Christian research nonprofit organization, have found that a quarter of U.S. Christians, including 10 percent of all born-again Christians, embrace the idea. Remarkably, recent surveys reveal that nearly sixty percent of Americans believe reincarnation is possible.

Furthermore, there have been many books published and much research done on the subject of people's subconscious memories of past lives and even memories of the time in between two lives. Dr. Michael Newton explains, "that people under hypnosis are not dreaming or hallucinating— and in this state they are not capable of lying. They report whatever they see and hear in their subconscious minds as if everything is a literal observation. While, under hypnosis, it is possible for them to misinterpret something they are seeing, but they will not report on anything they do not feel to be the literal truth."

These are the stages that he described:

1. Death and departure – Most clients recall looking down at their body and seeing people mourning over their death. Some people reported staying around their loved ones until after their funeral. During this time, clients could feel a pull towards a light, and described a tunnel of sorts to get there.

2. Gateway to the spirit world – This is the stage where clients report moving through the tunnel and reaching the light at the end. Location of the tunnel varies, as some say it appears right above their bodies and others say they have to travel above the Earth to reach it. After reaching the end of the tunnel, clients almost always describe it in varying ways, beautiful visions, music, and scenery. Dr. Newton suggests that these images are beloved memories from our lives, to help give a feeling of familiarity during such an overwhelming process. Younger souls may feel sad or confused during this time, and it's reported that their guides will come to assist and comfort.

3. Homecoming – Here we are greeted by souls who are close to us. They appear as luminous beings who sometimes project faces of people who are still 'alive' in a physicality because our souls only project a certain percentage of itself into the physical body, so there will always be a part of the soul existing in the spirit realm. During this stage, the soul begins to remember more about the afterlife and also their previous lives, feeling more at ease with the process. Souls which have committed murder or suicide will analyze their actions with their guide and decide on an appropriate path to begin almost immediately.

4. Orientation – During the orientation stage, a soul will shed any regret, doubt, sadness, or traumatic memories from its previous life by going through what clients describe as a 'shower of light.' This renews the soul's vibrancy and restores it to its original vibration. Afterward, we discuss with our guide everything that has happened in our life and decides whether or not we lived up to our expectations about how we dealt with those incidents and if the lessons need to be repeated in the next life.

5. Transition – After we have completed our light shower and have worked through our previous life, we then move onto what most describe as the most breathtaking visions of the entire journey. Here we see a mega-hub of souls at the same stage, all moving through beautiful tunnels of light to their destination. Clients describe this moment as exciting because there is no

darkness, just pure light, and we are also on our way to meet up with our soul family, souls who are at a similar stage in their evolution and with whom we share our lives. Once we meet up with these souls, we usually compare experiences and learn from each other. These are souls that we keep reincarnating with over and over again, playing various roles with each other such as partners, brothers/sisters, parents, children, etc. Sometimes souls will be present but dimmer and quieter than others, and that is because they are still projecting a physicality at that moment. Another crucial aspect of this stage is to meet a grand council that oversees our previous life, going into more detail about the experiences and lessons learned.

6. Placement – This stage is almost like a school where larger groups of soul families (up to thousands) who incarnate around each other in cycles learn about their previous experiences. Here clients report projecting into specific scenes from their previous life and into other people's minds to gain a full understanding of the larger picture. Here we feel what others felt to learn how we hurt people in certain situations. This stage can also see the larger soul groups connecting in circles, sharing more ideas, singing, and experiencing other joyful events.

7. Life selection – During this stage we move to a large sphere of light where we then choose our next life path. We can see multiple paths and can temporarily project into these lives to feel which one would be most appropriate. We also have the ability to fast forward through the timelines to see critical events that will happen. Some souls will choose greater challenges to experience such as a disability or premature death.

8. Choosing a new body - This process is a part of the previous life selection stage but has a separate categorization because it focuses on the physical appearance that we will possess in the next life. This choice vastly affects our experience, so it usually takes much thought as to what it will be. If you were obese in one life, chances are you will choose to be skinny the next, etc.

9. Preparation and Embarkation – After choosing our life path, next we meet up with our soul group, the people who will play roles in the next life, to do extensive planning and to create synchronicities and cues that will guide us throughout our life. Higher-level guides also help to plan out specific symbols we will see or hear that will trigger certain thoughts and actions at specific times. After the synchronicities are decided, we once again meet with a counsel to go over our goals and plans for the next life. This meeting is also to encourage us to have patience, to hold true to our values, to trust ourselves in the midst of difficult situations, and to avoid indulging in anger and negativity.

10. Rebirth – Clients report traveling back to Earth through the same tunnel they left in, entering the mother's womb. Until the age of 5, the soul is able to leave the baby's body to travel and meet up with other souls if it wishes but will snap back to the body if the baby is in any turmoil. During the first few years, the soul will work to integrate its energy with the brain.

To illustrate the point, this outline of experiences between lives is based on four decades' worth of research, and like Dr. Newton and other hypnotherapists state, clients under such hypnotic states will never lie and will only describe what they are seeing. How is it that almost everyone who undergoes hypnotherapy or who have NDE or OOB experiences, regardless of whatever religious or cultural background they come from, report such similar experiences? Could it be merely coincidental? How is it that people recall these kinds of experiences after being declared clinically dead? These are the sorts of questions that can only be answered by the assimilation of science and spirituality.

References:

Credit goes to Collective Evolution for the majority of this article.

1. Lommel, Pim van. "About the Continuity of Our Consciousness," in Brain Death and Disorders of Consciousness, ed. C. Machado and D. A. Shewmon (New York: Kluwer Academic/ Plenum Publishers, 2004); Advances in Experimental Medicine

and Biology (2004) 550: 115-132, http://iands.org/research/
important-research-articles/43-dr-pim-van-lommel-md-
continuity-of-consciousness.html?start=2.

2. Newton, Michael. Journey of Souls: New Case Studies of Life
    Between Lives (Woodbury, MN: Llewellyn Publications, 1994),
    p. 2; http://spiritualregression.org/.

3. Wilcock, David. The Synchronicity Key: The Hidden
    Intelligence Guiding the Universe and You (Part II, Chapter 8:
    Mapping Out the Afterlife). Penguin Group US. Kindle Edition.
    http://www.collective-evolution.com/2013/10/29/science-
    now-proves-reincarnation-a-look-at-the-souls-journey-after-
    death/#sthash.6TnBUI6f.dpuf

    http://www.spiritscienceandmetaphysics.com/where-do-we-go-
    when-we-die-a-look-at-the-souls-journey-after-death/#sthash.
    BxWaaNxE.dpuf

L. Ron Hubbard, author of Dianetics and the founder of Scientology, introduced his own version of reincarnation into his new religion. According to Hubbard, past lives need auditing to get at the root of one's "troubles." He also claims that "Dianetics gave impetus to Bridey Murphy" and that some scientologists have been dogs and other animals in previous lives ("A Note on Past Lives" in The Rediscovery of the Human Soul). According to Hubbard, "It has only been in Scientology that the mechanics of death have been thoroughly understood." What happens in death is this: The Thetan (spirit) finds itself without a body (which has died) and then it goes looking for a new body. Thetans "will hang around people. They will see a woman who is pregnant and follow her down the street." Then, the Thetan will slip into the newborn "usually...two or three minutes after the delivery of a child from the mother. A Thetan usually picks it up about the time the baby takes its first gasp." How Hubbard knows this is never revealed. http://skepdic. com/reincarn.html

Christianity teaches that we only go around once and then you go on to meet your Maker. It teaches that one day Jesus will come and this world, as we know it, will end.

If this is true, then Hindus and Buddhist are wrong about reincarnation and a very nasty surprise awaits those who count on multiple do-overs, doesn't it?

VI

PSYCHIC EXPERIENCES

When I was about nine years old my father purchased a couple of lots in our little town with the intention of building a house for our family. He made a deal with a couple of farmers to tear down some old houses on their properties and we would get to keep the lumber from those houses to use in building our house.

In one of the houses was a child's highchair. When I saw it, I knew I had to have that highchair. It was very old fashioned with a rounded back and it did not have a tray, but for some unknown reason, I had to have that chair. I went to mother and asked her if I could put it in the trunk of the car and she gave me an emphatic "No." My heart was broken. I was used to her telling me no, but I had to have this particular highchair. I questioned her as to why and did something I did not usually do. I threw a huge tantrum and cried and carried on something awful. I explained over and over how I had to have it for my dolls, that I didn't have very many toys, and how it wouldn't take up much room, and how I would keep it out of the way. Nothing I said seemed to work until dad heard me. Dad said, "Let her have it." Then, of course, mom and dad proceeded to get into an argument, which I won't go into, but we left there that day with this old blue-painted highchair in the trunk of the car. All I could think about was my doll sitting in that old highchair.

I kept the highchair out of sight so as not to irritate mom or remind her of that day. I never really played with dolls, but my best doll sat in it.

A few months later when I was 10 or 11 and my sister was two years older, mother called my sister and me together one day and told us we were going to have a brother or a sister. All I could do was blurt out "I knew we needed that highchair." I happily relinquished my prized chair and dad found a tray some place for it, and from that time on the unborn baby became known as John Henry.

Sometimes you just know things. You do not know how you know, but as sure as you know a glass of water is a glass of water, you know things. My girlfriend and I went to play Bingo. We were standing in line waiting to purchase our cards and the lady behind me said, "I sure hope I win the coverall tonight." I don't know why, but it just popped out. I turned around and said, "Not tonight. Tonight, it's mine." My girlfriend laughed and said, "you're crazy." I said, "No, tonight I am going to win the coverall." Each game I hardly got a number and she said you better change your cards because your cards are lousy." I said, "that's okay, the only game that is important is the last one." I won the coverall game.

My husband and I had been waiting on a large check to come in for a couple of months. We were getting behind on our bills. I got up one morning and the thought came into my head "this is the day." I gathered the bills and the checkbook and took them to work with me. I wrote out the checks and stuck the paid bills in the mailbox. My husband called and said that the check came in. I said, "Yes, I know. I mailed out the bills." He said, "you've got a lot of nerve."

My parents were visiting and dinner was ready. My husband was not home yet. Mom said, "Aren't you going to wait for Ned?" I said, "No?" We went ahead with dinner without him. I just felt he would not be joining us for dinner and I was right.

My husband and I were invited to visit some people I had never met. While I was bathing and getting ready I was asking my husband about them and all his answers were, "I don't know." Suddenly it dawned on me and I said, "I'll bet they're wife swappers." I don't know how I knew that or why I said it. They were. We arrived at their house and the wife took my husband's arm and guided him to one couch and her husband guided me to sit on another couch. I can't believe my husband exposed me to that. I am sure he knew ahead of time and wanted to see my reaction.

When I met my first husband, someone else asked me out on a date and I told them "thank you but I have met someone that I am going to marry." A couple months later my then husband proposed.

After I was divorced, I was on my way home from work one night and something kept telling me to stop at a certain casino. I was being told to go inside the front door of the casino to the left and there would be dollar machines and I would be told which machine to play, but not to play less than three dollars at a time. I had gambled before, but I had never played dollar machines. However, this voice kept nagging at me and I could not ignore it. I went in and bought twenty dollars in silver. In those days you actually played coins and you got real silver dollars. I wish I had some of them now. I walked down the first aisle which really were dollar machines, and I stopped where I felt I was supposed to, and I sat down. Not being used to playing dollar machines I kept wanting to play one dollar, but each time something said to play the three at a time. Why I was not compelled to play five I do not know. There was a guy next to me playing and he was playing five. I was hitting a pair now and then and three of a kind now and then – enough to keep me going on my $20. All of a sudden, I hit a royal flush for $750.00. The guy next to me was completely disgusted because I did not have five coins in to hit for four thousand dollars. I was told to play three coins and I did. I cashed out, stuck the money in an envelope, and mailed it to my father and mother.

A couple of days later I called and talked to my father to see if he had received it. Dad said their furnace had gone out and they had been praying because they did not know where they were going to get the money to pay for a new furnace and a new furnace would cost them $750.00.

There were many similar experiences involving my parents. Dad told me they would need a certain amount of money or they would be short a certain amount of money and he would pray about it and he would always get a letter in the mail with that amount of money in it from me. Now my parents are gone and I haven't made a bet of any kind in over 28 years.

Most of my experiences I just take or took for granted. They become part of my everyday life and I don't really think about them as being any different from anyone else. You think of it as listening to your gut or your instincts and everyone can do that.

When I was married the first time I believe my extra-sensory perception was at its highest. I think it was because I was the main bread winner of the family and had to take on more responsibility. Whenever the phone would ring if I was busy cooking, I would tell my husband, "that's so and so. Tell her such and such." He would pick up the phone and say, "Hi (name), Irene said to tell you …." They would gulp and say something like, "well, I guess that answers my question," and hang up on him. He always thought it was funny, but I don't think my friends did.

Some say these are psychic experiences. Some say they are coincidences. Some say they are just gut instincts. Some say they are intuitions. Some say they are having faith in a higher power. Some say you are being on a different wave link. Some say God answers prayers. What do you think?

What about when you listen to your gut and take a different route to work some morning and find out you avoided an accident? Not long ago I decided at the last second to pull into a 7-11 store just before my light turned red and as I turned in, a car ran through the light and would have hit me had I kept going, because he hit the car beside me instead.

VII

THE BIBLE AND PSYCHICS

The Old Testament warns against consulting with mediums and psychics in several instances. These practices are considered detestable to the Lord.

The Bible is full of scriptures warning of mediums and psychics and man's use of their practices.

Leviticus 19:31 "Do not turn to mediums or seek out spiritists, for you will be defiled by them. I am the Lord your God." (NIV)

Leviticus 20:27 "A man also or woman that hath a familiar spirit, or that is a wizard, shall surely be put to death: they shall stone them with stones: their blood shall be upon them."

Deuteronomy 18:10-13 10 "There shall not be found among you any one that maketh his son or his daughter to pass through the fire, or that useth divination, or an observer of times, or an enchanter, or a witch. 11 Or a charmer, or a consulter with familiar spirits, or a wizard, or a necromancer. 12 For all that do these things are an abomination unto the Lord: and because of these abominations the Lord thy God doth drive them out from before thee. 13 Thou shalt be perfect with the Lord thy God."

1 Chronicles 10:13-14 13 "Saul died because he was unfaithful to the Lord; he did not keep the word of the Lord and even consulted a medium for guidance and did not inquire of the Lord. So, the Lord put him to death and turned the kingdom over to David, son of Jesse." (NIV)

2 Chronicles 33:6 "He [King Manasseh] sacrificed his sons in the fire in the Valley of Ben Hinnom, practiced sorcery, divination, and witchcraft, and consulted mediums and spiritists. He did much evil in the eyes of the Lord, provoking him to anger." (NIV)

There was a time in my life when I read Tarot cards. I was good at it, and it made me feel special. I read only for a short time because I soon learned that people have a need to live their lives by something other than by their natural abilities. They need to feel unique, and they needed to feel in control wanting to know what is going on before it happens so they can control the events around them. I had friends call me every day because they wanted to know what the cards said about them that day or what was going to happen that day. I felt uneasy about that. When your friends are not calling you for readings, they are picking up the newspaper and reading their horoscope every day. They cannot just get up and let their day happen freely and let God control their life. If you look at Facebook, your friends are checking out their horoscopes and posting your horoscope for you.

When I started reading the Bible and saw what the Bible said about Spiritists, I stopped reading Tarot and threw away the cards.

It does not mean I do not believe that some of the Mediums that are out there today are not authentic. I have watched some on TV that I believe are genuine in their communication with the dead. And I do believe that you can communicate with the spirits after they have moved into the afterlife. I just believe you are not supposed to. There is a reason God said not to do it.

I believe people must put their faith in God, not in Tarot cards, or the stars, or spirits, or those that have moved into the afterlife. There is a reason that God said "Do not turn to mediums, or seek out spiritists, for you will be defiled by them. I am the Lord your God." There is a danger involved.

Over the years, traditional cards came under pressure from the Catholic Church. The trumps representing the Pope, Female Pope, Empress, and Emperor, were often replaced. The church regarded such cards to be against the doctrine of providence. In 1432, the cards were denounced as the creation of Satan. The 1570s saw further backlash for the cards as the Church attacked gambling and theater as they were seen to be promoting false gods and idols. However, Tarot cards were often exempt from bans and were a fixture in upper-class society.

Antoine Court de Gēbelin Tarot cards were first used on a more spiritual level around 1781. Swiss occult writer, clergyman, and Freemason Antoine Court de Gēbelin wrote of Tarot cards in his book on civilization. De Gebelin theorized that the cards were the key to lost Egyptian magical wisdom written by Thoth, the Egyptian God of inspired written knowledge and that the cards hid information on the structure of the world that had been hidden in a game of Egyptian priests to avoid the loss of their knowledge.

The first known fortune-teller to have used Tarot cards is Jean-Baptiste Alliette ("Etteilla,") from Paris. He designed cards that showed possible future events such as travel, sadness, love, and fortune. Alliette was the first to publish divinatory meanings for the cards.

And then in 1856, a famous occultist known as Eliphas Lévi, developed a parallel between the Tarot and the Kabbalah: The Hebrew system of mysticism. This stimulated a new belief that the Tarot may have originated in Israel and contained the wisdom of the Tree of Life. The new theory brought all 78 cards together as keys to the mysteries, but, of course, there were no facts to support it. Nevertheless, from this point forward, many magical and esoteric groups recognized the Tarot as a timeless body of knowledge that had significance in every mystical path, and it has been linked with almost every magical system or religion known to humankind.

There are still only two options open to us when we die. Heaven or Hell. We have a choice of where we want to spend eternity.

Is there a purgatory? Catholic theology Purgatory is said to be a place that a Christian's soul goes to after death to be cleansed of the sins that had not been fully satisfied during life. There is nothing in the Bible that suggests that there is a purgatory. This whole idea is based on salvation by work and not on salvation by faith in the sacrifice that Jesus died for us. That idea that we can earn heaven by works is not biblical. The apostle Paul clearly indicated that in Ephesians 2:8-9 "It is by grace you have been saved, through faith -- and this not from yourselves, it is the gift of God -- not by works so that no one can boast." NIV http://www.tnnonline.net/theonews/heaven-hell/state-dead/)

The primary Scriptural passage Catholics point to for evidence of Purgatory is 1 Corinthians 3:15, which says, "If it is burned up, he will suffer loss; he himself will be saved, but only as one escaping through the flames." The passage (1 Corinthians 3:12-15) is using an illustration of things going through fire as a description of believers' works being judged. If our works are of good quality "gold, silver, costly stones," they will pass through the fire unharmed, and we will be rewarded for them. If our works are of poor quality "wood, hay, and straw," they will be consumed by the fire, and there will be no reward. The passage does not say that believers pass through the fire, but rather that a believer's works pass through the fire. 1 Corinthians 3:15 refers to the believer "escaping through the flames," not "being cleansed by the flames." http://www.gotquestions.org/purgatory.html

The whole idea of purgatory is strictly a Catholic creed. Catholics believe all Christians, except Saints, will spend time in purgatory until they are purified and worthy of Heaven. This teaching contradicts the gospel that Jesus, by his atoning death has fully atoned for our sins and bore our punishment (Isaiah 53:4 "Surely he hath borne our griefs and carried our sorrows: yet we did esteem him stricken, smitten of God, and afflicted. 5. But he was wounded for our transgressions, he was bruised for our iniquities: the chastisement of our peace was upon him, and with his stripes we are healed. 6. All we like sheep have gone astray; we have turned everyone to his own way, and the Lord hath laid on him the iniquity of us all."); and that all earthly punishment ends at death.

The whole chapter of Luke 16 explains it clearly. You believe in Jesus and go to heaven; you do not, and you go to hell. John 14:6 6. Jesus answered, "I am the way and the truth and the life. No one comes to the Father except through me." (NIV)

The Bible clearly says that man is made up of three parts: Spirit, Soul, and Body. 1 Thess. 5:23-24 "May your whole spirit, soul and body be kept blameless at the coming of our Lord Jesus Christ." NIV

The spirit and soul are independent of each other even though they work in harmony.

Bible Verses about what happens when you die:

Daniel 12:2 – "And many of them that sleep in the dust of the earth shall awake, some to everlasting life, and some to shame [and] everlasting contempt."

1 Thessalonians 4:13-18 – "But I would not have you to be ignorant, brethren, concerning them which are asleep, that ye sorrow not, even as others which have no hope."

2 Corinthians 5:10 – "For we must all appear before the judgment seat of Christ; that every one may receive the things [done] in [his] body, according to that he hath done, whether [it be] good or bad."

Ecclesiastes 12:7 – "Then shall the dust return to the earth as it was: and the spirit shall return unto God who gave it."

Ezekiel 18:4 - "Behold, all souls are mine; as the soul of the father, so also the soul of the son is mine: the soul that sinneth, it shall die."

Ecclesiastes 9:5 – "For the living know that they shall die: but the dead know not anything, neither have they any more a reward; for the memory of them is forgotten."

Revelation 21:4 – "And God shall wipe away all tears from their eyes; and there shall be no more death, neither sorrow, nor crying, neither shall there be any more pain: for the former things are passed away."

1 Corinthians 15:51 – "Behold, I shew you a mystery; We shall not all sleep, but we shall all be changed,"

Romans 2:6-8 – "6 Who will render to every man according to his deeds: 7 To them who by patient continuance in well doing seek for glory and honour and immortality, eternal life: 8 But unto them that are contentious, and do not obey the truth, but obey unrighteousness, indignation and wrath,"

Psalms 127:4 – "As arrows [are] in the hand of a mighty man; so [are] children of the youth."

1 Corinthians 11:1-2 – "Be ye followers of me, even as I also am of Christ. 2 Now I praise you, brethren, that ye remember me in all things, and keep the ordinances, as I delivered them to you."

Romans 6:23 - "For the wages of sin [is] death; but the gift of God [is] eternal life through Jesus Christ our Lord."

Revelation 20:15 – "Lord himself shall descend from heaven with a shout, with the voice of the archangel, and with the trump of God: and the dead in Christ shall rise first:"

John 5:24 – "Verily, verily, I say unto you, He that heareth my word, and believeth on him that sent me, hath everlasting life, and shall not come into condemnation; but is passed from death unto life."

Matthew 10:28 – "And fear not them which kill the body but are not able to kill the soul: but rather fear him which is able to destroy both soul and body in hell."

James 2:26 – "For as the body without the spirit is dead, so faith without works is dead also."

John 6:50-71 – "This is the bread which cometh down from heaven, that a man may eat thereof, and not die. 51 I am the living bread which came down from heaven: if any man eat of this bread, he shall live forever: and the bread that I will give is my flesh, which I will give for the life of the world. 52 The Jews therefore strove among themselves, saying, how can this man give us his flesh to eat? 53 Then Jesus said unto them, Verily, verily, I say unto you, except ye eat the flesh of the Son of man, and drink his blood, ye have no life in you. 54 Whoso eateth my flesh, and drinketh my blood, hath eternal life; and I will raise him up at the last day. 55 For my flesh is meat indeed, and my blood is drink indeed. 56 He that eateth my flesh, and drinketh my blood, dwelleth in me, and I in him. 57 As the living Father hath sent me, and I live by the Father: so he that eateth me, even he shall live by me. 58 This is that bread which came down from heaven: not as your fathers did eat manna and are dead: he that eateth of this bread shall live forever. 59 These things said he in the synagogue, as he taught in Capernaum. 60 Many therefore of his disciples, when they had heard this, said, this is an hard saying; who can hear it? 61 When Jesus knew in himself that his disciples murmured at it, he said unto them, Doth this offend you? 62 What and if ye shall see the Son of man ascend up where he was before? 63 It is the spirit that quickeneth; the flesh profiteth nothing: the words that I speak unto you, they are spirit, and they are life. 64 But there are some of you that believe not. For Jesus knew from the beginning who they were that believed not, and who should betray him. 65 And he said, therefore said I unto you, that no man can come unto me, except it were given unto him of my Father. 66 From that time many of his disciples went back and walked no more with him. 67 Then said Jesus unto the twelve, will ye also go away? 68 Then Simon Peter answered him, Lord, to whom shall we go? thou hast the words of eternal life. 69 And we believe and are sure that thou art that Christ, the Son of the living God. 70 Jesus answered them, have not I chosen you twelve, and one of you is a devil? 71 He spake of Judas Iscariot the son of Simon: for he it was that should betray him, being one of the twelve."

Philippians 1:21 – "For to me to live [is] Christ, and to die [is] gain."

Romans 14:10 – "But why dost thou judge thy brother? or why dost thou set at nought thy brother? for we shall all stand before the judgment seat of Christ."

Acts 2:29 – "Men [and] brethren, let me freely speak unto you of the patriarch David, that he is both dead and buried, and his sepulchre is with us unto this day."

Genesis 2:7 – "And the Lord God formed man [of] the dust of the ground and breathed into his nostrils the breath of life; and man became a living soul."

1 Peter 4:6 – "For this cause was the gospel preached also to them that are dead, that they might be judged according to men in the flesh, but live according to God in the spirit."

James 4:14 – "Whereas ye know not what [shall be] on the morrow. For what [is] your life? It is even a vapour, that appeareth for a little time, and then vanisheth away."

1 Thessalonians 4:13 – "But I would not have you to be ignorant, brethren, concerning them which are asleep, that ye sorrow not, even as others which have no hope."

Philippians 3:10 – "That I may know him, and the power of his resurrection, and the fellowship of his sufferings, being made conformable unto his death;"

1 Corinthians 15:22 – "For as in Adam all die, even so in Christ shall all be made alive."

Romans 8:28 – "And we know that all things work together for good to them that love God, to them who are the called according to [his] purpose."

John 11:25 – "Jesus said unto her, I am the resurrection, and the life: he that believeth in me, though he were dead, yet shall he live:"

John 5:29 – "And shall come forth; they that have done good, unto the resurrection of life; and they that have done evil, unto the resurrection of damnation."

Revelation 20:11-13 – "And I saw a great white throne, and him that sat on it, from whose face the earth and the heaven fled away; and there was found no place for them. 12 And I saw the dead, small and great, stand before God; and the books were opened: and another book was opened, which is the book of life: and the dead were judged out of those things which were written in the books, according to their works. 13 And the sea gave up the dead which were in it; and death and hell delivered up the dead which were in them: and they were judged every man according to their works."

Revelation 20:5 – "But the rest of the dead lived not again until the thousand years were finished. This [is] the first resurrection."

Revelation 1:18 – "I [am] he that liveth, and was dead; and, behold, I am alive for evermore, Amen; and have the keys of hell and of death."

Hebrews 9:27 – "And as it is appointed unto men once to die, but after this the judgment:"

1 Thessalonians 4:17 – "Then we which are alive [and] remain shall be caught up together with them in the clouds, to meet the Lord in the air: and so shall we ever be with the Lord."

2 Corinthians 5:8 – "We are confident, [I say], and willing rather to be absent from the body, and to be present with the Lord.

Romans 1:24 – "Wherefore God also gave them up to uncleanness through the lusts of their own hearts, to dishonour their own bodies between themselves:"

Acts 2:34 – "For David is not ascended into the heavens: but he saith himself, The Lord said unto my Lord, Sit thou on my right hand,"

Acts 2:31 – "He seeing this before spake of the resurrection of Christ, that his soul was not left in hell, neither his flesh did see corruption."

Acts 2:27 – "Because thou wilt not leave my soul in hell, neither wilt thou suffer thine Holy One to see corruption."

John 21:1-25 – "After these things Jesus shewed himself again to the disciples at the sea of Tiberias; and on this wise shewed he [himself]."

John 20:1-31 – "The first [day] of the week cometh Mary Magdalene early, when it was yet dark, unto the sepulchre, and seeth the stone taken away from the sepulchre. 2 Then she runneth, and cometh to Simon Peter, and to the other disciple, whom Jesus loved, and saith unto them, They have taken away the Lord out of the sepulchre, and we know not where they have laid him. 3 Peter therefore went forth, and that other disciple, and came to the sepulchre. 4 So they ran both together: and the other disciple did outrun Peter and came first to the sepulchre. 5 And he stooping down, and looking in, saw the linen clothes lying; yet went he not in. 6 Then cometh Simon Peter following him, and went into the sepulchre, and seeth the linen clothes lie, 7 And the napkin, that was about his head, not lying with the linen clothes, but wrapped together in a place by itself. 8 Then went in also that other disciple, which came first to the sepulchre, and he saw, and believed. 9 For as yet they knew not the scripture, that he must rise again from the dead. 10 Then the disciples went away again unto their own home. 11 But Mary stood without at the sepulchre weeping: and as she wept, she stooped down, and looked into the sepulchre; 12 And seeth two angels in white sitting, the one at the head, and the other at the feet, where the body of Jesus had lain. 13 And they say unto her, Woman, why weepest thou? She saith unto them, because they have taken away my Lord, and I know not where they have laid him. 14 And when she had thus said, she turned herself back, and saw Jesus standing, and knew not that it was Jesus. 15 Jesus saith unto her, Woman, why weepest thou? whom seekest thou? She, supposing him to be the gardener, saith unto him, Sir, if thou have borne him hence, tell me where thou hast laid him, and I will take him away. 16 Jesus saith unto her, Mary. She turned herself, and saith unto him, Rabboni; which is to say, Master. 17 Jesus saith unto her, Touch me not; for I am not yet ascended to my Father: but go to my brethren, and say unto them, I ascend unto my Father, and your Father; and to my God, and your God. 18 Mary Magdalene came and told the disciples that she had seen the Lord, and that he had spoken these things unto her. 19 Then the same day at evening, being the first day of the week, when the doors were shut where the disciples were assembled for fear of the Jews, came Jesus and stood in the midst, and saith unto them, Peace be unto you. 20 And when he had so said, he shewed unto them his hands and his side. Then were the disciples glad, when they saw the Lord. 21 Then said Jesus to them again, Peace be unto you: as my Father hath sent me, even so send I you. 22 And when he had said this, he breathed on them, and saith unto them, receive ye the Holy Ghost: 23 Whosesoever sins ye remit, they are remitted unto them; and whosesoever sins ye retain, they are retained. 24 But Thomas, one of the twelve, called Didymus, was not with them when Jesus came. 25 The other disciples therefore said unto him, we have seen the Lord. But he said unto them, Except I shall see in his hands the print of the nails and put my finger into the print of the nails, and thrust my hand into his side, I will not believe. 26 And after eight days again his disciples were within, and Thomas with them: then came Jesus, the doors being shut, and stood in the midst, and said, Peace be unto you. 27 Then saith he to Thomas, reach hither thy finger, and behold my hands; and reach hither thy hand, and thrust it into my side: and be not faithless, but believing. 28 And Thomas answered and said unto him, My Lord and my God. 29 Jesus saith unto him, Thomas, because thou hast seen me, thou hast believed: blessed are they that have not seen, and yet have believed. 30 And many other signs truly did Jesus in the presence of his disciples, which are not written in this book: 31 But these are written, that ye might believe that Jesus is the

Christ, the Son of God; and that believing ye might have life through his name."

John 3:16 – "For God so loved the world, that he gave his only begotten Son, that whosoever believeth in him should not perish, but have everlasting life."

Ezekiel 18:20 – "The soul that sinneth, it shall die. The son shall not bear the iniquity of the father, neither shall the father bear the iniquity of the son: the righteousness of the righteous shall be upon him, and the wickedness of the wicked shall be upon him."

Isaiah 3:1-26 - "For, behold, the Lord, the Lord of hosts, doth take away from Jerusalem and from Judah the stay and the staff, the whole stay of bread, and the whole stay of water. 2 The mighty man, and the man of war, the judge, and the prophet, and the prudent, and the ancient, 3 The captain of fifty, and the honourable man, and the counsellor, and the cunning artificer, and the eloquent orator. 4 And I will give children to be their princes, and babes shall rule over them. 5 And the people shall be oppressed, everyone by another, and every one by his neighbour: the child shall behave himself proudly against the ancient, and the base against the honourable. 6 When a man shall take hold of his brother of the house of his father, saying, Thou hast clothing, be thou our ruler, and let this ruin be under thy hand: 7 In that day shall he swear, saying, I will not be an healer; for in my house is neither bread nor clothing: make me not a ruler of the people. 8 For Jerusalem is ruined, and Judah is fallen: because their tongue and their doings are against the Lord, to provoke the eyes of his glory. 9 The shew of their countenance doth witness against them; and they declare their sin as Sodom, they hide it not. Woe unto their soul! for they have rewarded evil unto themselves. 10 Say ye to the righteous, that it shall be well with him: for they shall eat the fruit of their doings. 11 Woe unto the wicked! it shall be ill with him: for the reward of his hands shall be given him. 12 As for my people, children are their oppressors, and women rule over them. O my people, they which lead thee cause thee to err, and destroy the way of thy paths. 13 The Lord standeth up to plead, and standeth to judge the people. 14 The Lord will enter into judgment with the ancients of his people, and the princes thereof:

for ye have eaten up the vineyard; the spoil of the poor is in your houses. 15 What mean ye that ye beat my people to pieces and grind the faces of the poor? saith the Lord God of hosts. 16 Moreover the Lord saith, Because the daughters of Zion are haughty, and walk with stretched forth necks and wanton eyes, walking and mincing as they go, and making a tinkling with their feet: 17 Therefore the Lord will smite with a scab the crown of the head of the daughters of Zion, and the Lord will discover their secret parts. 18 In that day the Lord will take away the bravery of their tinkling ornaments about their feet, and their cauls, and their round tires like the moon, 19 The chains, and the bracelets, and the mufflers, 20 The bonnets, and the ornaments of the legs, and the headbands, and the tablets, and the earrings, 21 The rings, and nose jewels, 22 The changeable suits of apparel, and the mantles, and the wimples, and the crisping pins, 23 The glasses, and the fine linen, and the hoods, and the vails. 24 And it shall come to pass, that instead of sweet smell there shall be stink; and instead of a girdle a rent; and instead of wellset hair baldness; and instead of a stomacher a girding of sackcloth; and burning instead of beauty. 25 Thy men shall fall by the sword, and thy mighty in the war. 26 And her gates shall lament and mourn; and she being desolate shall sit upon the ground."

Revelation 20:11-15 – "And I saw a great white throne, and him that sat on it, from whose face the earth and the heaven fled away; and there was found no place for them. 12 And I saw the dead, small and great, stand before God; and the books were opened: and another book was opened, which is the book of life: and the dead were judged out of those things which were written in the books, according to their works. 13 And the sea gave up the dead which were in it; and death and hell delivered up the dead which were in them: and they were judged every man according to their works. 14 And death and hell were cast into the lake of fire. This is the second death. 15 And whosoever was not found written in the book of life was cast into the lake of fire."

Revelation 20:6 – "Blessed and holy [is] he that hath part in the first resurrection: on such the second death hath no power, but they shall be priests of God and of Christ and shall reign with him a thousand years."

Revelation 6:9 – "And when he had opened the fifth seal, I saw under the altar the souls of them that were slain for the word of God, and for the testimony which they held:"

1 Peter 1:3 – "Blessed [be] the God and Father of our Lord Jesus Christ, which according to his abundant mercy hath begotten us again unto a lively hope by the resurrection of Jesus Christ from the dead,"

1 Timothy 6:15 – "Which in his times he shall shew, [who is] the blessed and only Potentate, the King of kings, and Lord of Lords;"

Philippians 1:23 – "For I am in a strait betwixt two, having a desire to depart, and to be with Christ; which is far better:"

Romans 2:7 – "To them who by patient continuance in well doing seek for glory and honour and immortality, eternal life:"

John 5:25 – "Verily, verily, I say unto you, the hour is coming, and now is, when the dead shall hear the voice of the Son of God: and they that hear shall live."

Psalms 98:2 – "The LORD hath made known his salvation: his righteousness hath he openly shewed in the sight of the heathen.'"

1 John 5:12 – "He that hath the Son hath life; [and] he that hath not the Son of God hath not life."

1 Timothy 6:16 – "Who only hath immortality, dwelling in the light which no man can approach unto; whom no man hath seen, nor can see: to whom [be] honour and power everlasting. Amen."

Ecclesiastes 9:6 – "Also their love, and their hatred, and their envy, is now perished; neither have they any more a portion forever in any [thing] that is done under the sun."

Ecclesiastes 3:19-20 – "For that which befalleth the sons of men befalleth beasts; even one thing befalleth them: as the one dieth, so dieth the other; yea, they have all one breath; so that a man hath no preeminence above a beast: for all [is] vanity."

Psalms 49:15 – "But God will redeem my soul from the power of the grave: for he shall receive me. Selah."

Psalms 16:10 – "For thou wilt not leave my soul in hell; neither wilt thou suffer thine Holy One to see corruption."

Psalms 6:5 – "For in death [there is] no remembrance of thee: in the grave who shall give thee thanks?"

Genesis 3:19 – "In the sweat of thy face shalt thou eat bread, till thou return unto the ground; for out of it wast thou taken: for dust thou [art], and unto dust shalt thou return."
http://www.kingjamesbibleonline.org/Bible-Verses-About-What-Happens-When-You-Die/

Does that mean the ability to see into the future does not exist or does it just mean, as the Bible says, that God is a jealous God, and we should only be honoring Him, because after all, that is why we were put here on earth.

Tarot cards are not meant to tell your fortune or future. According to The Hermetic Order of the Golden Dawn, "The most powerful sources of information come from within and Tarot aids in coming in contact with one's Higher Self." There are 78 cards in a pack of Tarot cards, each with a different meaning. You do not have to be a psychic to read Tarot cards. To read Tarot cards, you must remain neutral and positive. You can give an open reading which addresses the larger aspect of life, or you can do a question reading that addresses a specific question that is asked.

Carl Jung said, "Things we might see as coincidence are actually signs that can help us make decisions and guide our lives -- if we recognize them."

The questions you have about your life (usually the reason for consulting the Tarot in the first place) are projected onto the pictures on the Tarot cards, so you divine answers from what you see. In this way, the Tarot is useful in helping you to tap into our subconscious to find answers that you might never consciously think about. Most readers have opposing ideas about how or why the Tarot works. Traditional Tarot Cards were first seen in Europe in 1375, having been brought over by the Islamic societies where they had been used for centuries before that. The first decks were created as a game.

Attempting to discover the future through reading tarot cards, palm reading, playing with the Ouija board, or some other form of fortunetelling, or even to try to control the future through black magic, witchcraft or sorcery violates the First Commandment. Bear in mind that fortunetelling is integrally linked with the practices of the occult.

VIII

SPIRIT GUIDES, ANGELS SERAPHIMS AND CHERUBIMS

Guardian Angels

Guardian Angels are pure love and sent to us to watch over us and help us. They bring to us only what will help us, protect us, guide us, and encourage us to desire only the qualities of our soul. They are with us before our conception when we are in soul form, and they accompany us through birth and are with us in our every thought, word and event we experience in life. They are committed to us for the entire journey of our life; they never leave us, and we are their only occupation. They will be with us when we leave this life and when we are, again, a soul in heaven.

Every person has, at least, two Guardian Angels. If you have patience and the desire, you can learn to communicate with them. It also takes some sensing, a lot of listening and some hearing to know their names. You can communicate with them. They will hear you. Talk to them as you do your very best friends. Guardian Angels also coordinate other angel teams that help with other aspects of your life.

The Guardian Angel concept is clearly present in the Old Testament, and its development is well marked. The Old Testament conceived of God's angels as his ministers who carried out his behests, and who were at times given special commissions, regarding men and mundane affairs.

Everyone has, at least, one Guardian Angel, with no exception. This is the angel who constantly stays with you, from birth until your transition back to heaven. This angel's love for you is unconditional. Your Guardian Angel makes certain you are always safe and guided. Our Guardian Angels can reveal themselves in any number of disguises, at any age, and in all shapes and skin colors. You see, contrary to popular belief, guardian angels don't necessarily appear in white flowing gowns with golden hair and big beautiful white feathered wings. Angels and Guardian Angels are the only spirit beings that can appear in human form. Sometimes they just look like normal people. Children have a far greater chance of connecting and interacting with their guardian angels than adults do because their hearts are so open, and their spirits are so strong. Adults are not as opened minded.

Communicating with your Guardian Angel is not difficult, and there is no magic formula. You just talk to them. They are not allowed to interfere, and they won't offer help to us unless we ask and then they only suggest. Pose a question to them before you go to bed and you will receive an answer either in your dreams, or you will just know the answer the next morning.

You can feel an angel's presence. You might just feel a warmth in your body. Perhaps you will feel a warm brush across your hand, your arm, your shoulder, or across your cheek. You may see a sparkle of white light out of the corner of your eye or hear a whisper in your ear.

When a near tragedy is averted, and you call it divine intervention, it was probably your guardian angel.

Angels

Angels have never been human. Angels are pure beings of light sent by God to guide, support, and give us unconditional love. They respond to our calls for guidance, assistance, protection, and comfort. God's thoughts of love create Angels. The word Angel means "Messenger of God." Angels love everyone unconditionally. They look past the surface and only see the good within all of us. They focus on our potential and not our faults. Angels are not judgmental, and they only bring love into our lives. You can ask for as many angels as you want to surround and protect you, your loved ones, your pets, and your home. Angels receive great joy from helping us, and they ask only that we occasionally remember to say, "Thank you" in gratitude for their help.

Angels, as opposed to Archangels or Seraphim or Cherubims, are closer to the material world and humans. The Catholics believe the angels are intercessors between us and God, that the angels deliver our prayers to God and that God then delivers the answer back to us through angels.

In Genesis 18-19, angels not only act as the executors of God's wrath against the cities of the plain, but they delivered Lot from danger; in Exodus 32:34, God says to Moses: "my angel shall go before thee." At a much later period, we have the story of Tobias, which might serve for a commentary on the words of Psalm 91:11: "For he will command his angels concerning you to guard you in all your ways;" (Cf. Psalm 33:8 and 34:5)

The belief that angels can be guides and intercessors for men can be found in Job 33:23, and in Daniel 10:13 angels seem to be assigned to certain countries. In this latter case, the "prince of the kingdom of Persia" contends with Gabriel. The same verse mentions "Michael, one of the chief princes."

Angels are without gender. Although Angels may seem to man to be more masculine or feminine if they appear to us at all, they are in essence genderless; it is their energy which contributes to their more masculine or feminine appearance.

Spirit Guides

"Guardian angels are sometimes confused with "Spirit Guides." A Spirit Guide is a loving being who has lived upon the earth in human form. They may have known you in this lifetime. Unlike angels who are without gender, Spirit Guides may be male or female. They receive special training in Heaven about how to become a spirit guide. This training emphasizes that they are to guide you but not to interfere with your free will or make decisions for you. They are there to give you general advice, comfort, and at times warning and protection. Most Spirit Guardians are someone that we were once related to.

"You can ask your angels and guides for help with anything and everything. There is nothing too big or too small to ask your angels to help you with. Remember that an angel or spirit guide will never tell you what to do. They will make suggestions that come via knowing, gut instincts and synchronicities, but they will never violate your free will. You can listen to their suggestions or ignore them. In either case, they will continue to guide you with unconditional love. Your angels and guides never give up on you!" http://angelwhispers.net/2012/10/angels-guardian-fangels-and-spirit-guides/

These types of angels and guardian angels are known as Ishim, or Ashim. They are intermediaries between God and humanity. They are the protective spirits of individuals and lands.

"We have several different types of guides depending on the culture you come from. Metaphysically speaking there are 4 basic categories or types of guides:

'The Relative Guide
'This is usually a person who knew you in this lifetime. They are the relative who helps you through day-to-day situations. They are the soul who greets you at the door when your time comes from 'transition' from life to death.
'The Spirit Guide
'This is usually a person you knew in a past life. Or it might be a Power Animal. Someone who is on the same spiritual level as yourself. This soul helps you with your higher purpose or mission in this embodiment. The karmic issues, the spiritual lessons, the gifts and talents you brought from the past into this life and so on. Their main purpose is to help you evolve your soul during this incarnation and to learn and grow.

'The Angels

'Everyone has a Guardian Angel watching over them, protecting them and providing a connection to the higher Divine Force. Angels are rarely incarnated beings. They are 'of the stars' and are the messengers of the Divine.
'The Master Teacher

'Our Master Guide joins with us at birth and stays by our side right through our lives until we pass on. This Guide gives us direction or emphasis. At different times in our lives, depending on the situation and lesson(s) we have to learn, we have new guides join us to provide guidance and insight into the situation.

'If there is a change in life direction or emphasis, the Master Guide will step back and these other guides will come forward. These guides can come in unexpected forms. You will also have with you, at the appropriate time, a Master Teacher. This soul is someone who is on a higher spiritual plane than yourself." http://theangelwhispers.org/spiritguides.html

Archangels

These are angels that supervise Guardian Angels and Angels on Earth – kind of like managers of the earthly hierarchy. You can call upon an Archangel whenever you need immediate assistance and most powerful assistance. Angels have no time or space limitations. For instance, an archangel could help many people in many geographical locations at the same time.

Because we are given free will, an angel can never intervene in our lives unless we ask them to. The only exception is if our life is in danger. Otherwise, we are free to invite constantly our angels or guardian angels into our lives to help us along.

In Matthew 18:10 of the Bible, Jesus Christ mentions that children have guardian angels protecting them.

Little children sometimes see their "spirit guides" and communicate with them. But grown-ups, being what they are, eventually convince the child that they are growing up and should not play silly games anymore. At that time, most children forget they have spirit playmates until their deathbeds, or there is a reason at another time in their life for the spirit guide to appear.

What do Spirit Guides do? They are assigned to us before we are born and nudge and guide us throughout our entire life. They do interfere in a good way if we pay attention. You know that gut feeling you get that you can't quite put your finger on? That might be a Spirit Guide poking you in the gut, so following your gut feeling is probably a good idea. A Spirit Guide can be an old soul from any culture, era or geographical location who is able to help us while we are in physical form.

What about when something tells you to go in a different direction when you go to work today, and you found out later there had been a bad accident on the road you usually take. Or how about if something told you to slow down, and a couple of blocks ahead you saw a cop with his radar out, or perhaps you decided to stop and get a cup of coffee on the way to work, and because you did, you avoided an accident just up the road. Perhaps these were just your Guides sending you flashes of intuition and information and saving you undue and unnecessary inconveniences.

All the people that survived 9/11 by being late for work that morning had a Spirit Guide story to tell. One told of having a blister on his heel from a new pair of shoes so he stopped at the drug store to get some Band-Aids. One lady called in because she stayed up late the night before to watch a football game. One guy takes a bus to work and the bus was late. There were many such stories and each person later struggled with "why me?" "Why was I saved when the others weren't?"

What about when you were thinking of someone you had not seen in 5 or so years and that very afternoon you ran into them at the mall? Was that coincidence, or did your Guides get together with their Guides and arrange a meeting? Guides can nudge you in the direction they want you to go. It just takes time and practice to be able to hear, see, or feel your Guides. Some guides are unique to you and others help you and help others as well. Each Guide is there for you for a different reason. Your main Guides will be with you for your entire lifetime.

One time in the early 1960's I was driving from Rock Island, Illinois across the state to Danville, Illinois. I was on what is now Interstate 74, but at that time it was a two-lane highway. It was around 3:00 a.m. It was pouring rain and I was entering a fairly sharp curve. I was going too fast, and I did the one thing you are not supposed to do -- I applied my brakes to slow down. My car started spinning out of control. Something told me to just let go of the steering wheel and take my foot off of the brake. I relaxed and let go. I closed my eyes and counted as my car whipped around the curve three and a half times, mostly backwards, and came to a halt. My car never once left the road. I was so fortunate. When the adrenalin stopped flowing, I opened my eyes and calmly turned my car around and resumed my journey, thanking the good Lord and the Angels or whoever was guiding my car that night. I believed it was divine intervention telling me to let go of the steering wheel and guiding my car around that curve until it stopped. I just sat back and relaxed and waited after I heard that voice. I did not attempt to control the vehicle myself. It was like the voice was talking directly into my ear and it was not a whisper or something I felt. It said "Let go of the wheel and relax." From there it was in God's hands.

Another time in the 1970's I had entered the on-ramp of Interstate 15 in downtown Las Vegas going toward Los Angeles. Again, it was raining, and the road was extremely slick. We don't often get rain in Las Vegas, so when we do the roads are very slick. The traffic was bumper to bumper and the guy in the car in front of me slammed on his brakes. When I applied my brakes, my car went into a slide into the curb, and I yelled, "Help" because there was only that 5 or 6-inch curb that kept me from going over the curb and onto the traffic on Interstate 95 below, a drop of about 30 or 40 feet. Fortunately, I just slid nicely along that curb and stopped. Again, I thanked whoever was guiding my car that day. And again, I call days like that "divine intervention."

Another time I was not in my car. I was at home cleaning the guest bathroom and the phone rang. I picked up the phone and leaned against the back of the tank of the toilet, and the tank cracked. Water started running all over the floor. I reached down in the back of the tank to turn off the water, but the faucet would not turn. I put down the phone and kept trying, and I could not get it to turn. I yelled, "Help Me." I reached down again and the faucet turned very easily so that I could shut off the water. To me, again, it was "divine intervention." You can call it what you like.

So, some say they don't interfere. I say if you ask, they will help you. If you lose something and you ask the angels to help you find it, they will help you find it. The next time you lose something, call upon your spirit guide or your guardian angel and ask them to help you find whatever it is that you lost and then think about something else for a while. It won't be long before you remember where you put the lost article.

Every one of us, from the moment of birth until the instant we end our corporeal existence, are in the presence of guides and/or guardian angels who wait for us and help us from the transition of our lives to life after we end our time here on earth. And we will always be met by those that preceded us into the next life who we loved the most. So you see it does not matter whether you are in a crowd, in a hospital, or out in the country all by yourself, you can never leave this life alone.

Always listen to your intuition, your gut instinct, your spirit guide; whatever you wish to call it. When you do not listen is when you start having complications in your life. One outstanding instance in my life was before my second marriage. I was being pressured to get married. I really did not want to get married since I had learned to enjoy my own company. There was also this gut nudge that I could not get rid of. There was something about marrying this man that I could not put my finger on. I loved him, and he seemed like a good person, but I always had this gut feeling that I should not marry him.

I discussed it with my father and he said, "always listen." He further said, "I don't think this is someone you should marry."

I thought about the situation for several weeks and finally decided that I would get married because I was doing it for the right reason. I did love him, and he treated me well.

Within a few weeks after our marriage, he began to change and decided I was his property, and it was okay for him to beat on me for no reason. And abusers do not need a reason. Had I known about abusers and the signs of abusive behavior, I would have known I was being stalked before my marriage. I was reminded of my previous instincts and the knowledge that you should always listen to your gut instincts. You may not know why at the time, but if you do listen, you will soon find out.

Angels are mentioned hundreds of times in the Bible. Most of the time they are referred to as "Angels of God."

Revelations 8:2 refers to seven angels that stood before the Lord. "2 And I saw the seven angels which stood before God, and to them were given seven trumpets."

These seven angels are Michael, Gabriel, and Raphael, the three named in the Bible, and Raguel, Remiel, Saraqael, and Uriel, named in Enoch 20:1-8, a book found in the Dead Sea Scrolls and the Bible of the Oriental Orthodox Church of Ethiopia.

"Michael, who leads all of the holy angels, often works on missions that involve fighting evil, proclaiming God's truth, and strengthening people's faith." Michael, one of the Holy Angels, namely the one put in charge of the best part of humankind, in charge of the nation. [Book of Enoch]

Saraqael, one of the Holy Angels; who is in charge of the spirits of men who cause the spirits to sin. [Book of Enoch]

'Gabriel, who communicates God's most important announcements to humans, specializes in helping people understand God's messages and apply them to their lives." Gabriel, one of the Holy Angels, who is in charge of the Serpents, and the Garden, and the Cherubim. [Book of Enoch]

'Raphael, who serves as God's main healing angel, cares for the health of people, animals, and every other part of God's creation.

'Uriel, who focuses on wisdom, often works on missions of helping people learn more about God, themselves, and others." Uriel, one of the Holy Angels; namely the Holy Angel of the Spirits of Men. [Book of Enoch]

Raguel, one of the Holy Angels; who takes vengeance on the world, and on the lights. [Book of Enoch]

"Believers have grouped these four leading angels into categories that correspond to their specialties on our planet: four directions (north, south, west, and east) and four natural elements (air, fire, water, and earth).

"Michael represents south and fire. As the angel of fire, Michael sparks a desire in people to discover spiritual truth and pursue closer relationships with God. He also helps people burn sins out of their lives as he works to protect them from evil. Michael empowers people to let go of fear and live with the passion of being on fire with love for the God who loves them.

'Gabriel represents west and water. As the angel of water, Gabriel inspires people to be receptive to God's messages. He also urges people to reflect on their thoughts and emotions and helps them clearly understand the messages within what they think and feel. Finally, Gabriel encourages people to pursue purity to move closer to God.

'Raphael represents east and air. As the angel of air, Raphael helps people break free of burdens, make healthy lifestyle choices, become the people God wants them to become, and soar toward the right goals for their lives.

'Uriel represents north and earth. As the angel of earth, Uriel grounds people in God's wisdom and gives them down-to-earth solutions for their problems. He also acts as stabilizing force in people's lives, helping them live at peace within themselves and in relationships with God and other people."
http://angels.about.com/od/MedicalMiracles/fl/Archangels-of-the-Four-Elements-in-Nature.htm

According to Enoch, there were four angels of the Lord Most High: "This first one, is the Holy Michael, the merciful and long-suffering. And the second, who is in charge of all the diseases, and in charge of all the wounds of the sons of men, is Raphael. And the third, who is in charge of all the powers, is the Holy Gabriel. And the fourth, who is in charge of repentance and hope of those who will inherit eternal life, is Phanuel. Enoch said those are the four angels of the Lord Most High that he heard in those days." [Enoch 40:9]

The angel that escorted Enoch to Heaven was called Haniel or Anafiel. It's interesting to note that the angels who encountered Enoch when he arrived in heaven detected the fact that he was a living human being by his scent and were upset about his presence there among the angels until God explained why he chose Enoch to come to heaven without dying first.

According to Enoch in the Book of Enoch, the names of the Holy Angels that keep watch are Uriel, the Holy Angel of the Spirits of Men; Raguel who takes vengeance on the world and on the lights; Michael who is put in charge of the best parts of the nation and humankind; Saraqael who is put in charge of the spirits of men who cause the spirit to sin; and Gabriel who is in charge of the Serpents, the Garden and the Cherubim.

In the Book of Enoch Chapter 69, Enoch was discussing the great flood with Holy Michael and which angels would participate. He named the following angels: Semyaza (Azza), Artaqifa, Armen, Kokabiel, Turiel, Ramiel, Daniel, Nuqael, Baraqiel, Azaziel, Armaros, Batriel, Basasael, Ananel, Turiel, Samsiel, Yetarel, Tumiel, another Turiel, Rumiel, and Azazel. 69.3 These are the leaders of hundreds, and the leaders of fifties, and the leaders of tens. 69.4 Yequn is the one that led astray all the children of the Holy Angels through the daughters of men. 69.5 Azbeel suggested an evil plan to the children of the Holy Angels so that they corrupted their bodies with the daughters of men. 69.6 Gadreel showed all the deadly blows to the sons of men and led Eve astray. Showed man how to make shields and breastplates, swords for slaughter and all weapons for death. 69.8 Penemue showed man all the secrets of their wisdom. He showed man how to write and from this man has gone astray to this day. Man should remain righteous and pure. 69.12 Kasdeyae shows all attacks on the womb and how to miscarry.

On four occasions, one angel specifically is referred to by name" Daniel (2 verses) 8:16 – "And I heard a man's voice between the banks of Ulai, which called, and said, Gabriel, make this man understand the vision. 9:21 - Yea, whiles I was speaking in prayer, even the man Gabriel, whom I had seen in the vision at the beginning, being caused to fly swiftly, touched me about the time of the evening oblation."

Luke (2 verses) 1:19 – "And the angel answering said unto him, I am Gabriel, that stand in the presence of God; and am sent to speak unto thee, and to shew thee these glad tidings." 1:26 – "And in the sixth month the angel Gabriel was sent from God unto a city of Galilee, named Nazareth,..."

Gabriel is best known for the Annunciation to Mary that she would be the Mother of Jesus, the Son of God (Luke 1:26-38). Gabriel is the only messenger mentioned in the Old Testament and foretold the births of John the Baptist and Jesus. He was sent to the City of Nazareth and told Mary that she would conceive in her womb and bear a son and call his name Jesus. In the Old Testament he appeared to Daniel, he inspired the writing of Genesis, and he was involved in the destruction of Sodom and Gomorrah.

According to legend, it will be Gabriel who will blow the horn at the time of the second coming of Christ. 1 Corinthians 15:52 "52 In a moment, in the twinkling of an eye, at the last trump: for the trumpet shall sound, and the dead shall be raised incorruptible, and we shall be changed."

Michael as one of the leading angels is considered "Prince" of the heavenly hosts and appears three times in the Book of Daniel (10:13, 10:21, and 12:1). He is the only one in the Bible referred to as an Archangel (Jude 1:9) and serves a major role in Chapter 12 of the Book of Revelation.

Michael is the field commander of God's Army. He is mentioned in the books of Daniel, Jude and Revelation where he leads God's armies against Satan's forces. He is generally referred to as St. Michael the Archangel.

Daniel 10:13 "But the prince of the kingdom of Persia withstood me one and twenty days: but, lo, Michael, one of the chief princes, came to help me; and I remained there with the kings of Persia."

Daniel 10:21 "21 But I will shew thee that which is noted in the scripture of truth: and there is none that holdeth with me in these things, but Michael your prince."

Daniel 12:1 "12 And at that time shall Michael stand up, the great prince which standeth for the children of thy people: and there shall be a time of trouble, such as never was since there was a nation even to that same time: and at that time thy people shall be delivered, every one that shall be found written in the book."

1 Thessalonians (1 verses) 4:16 – "For the Lord himself shall descend from heaven with a shout, with the voice of the archangel, and with the trump of God: and the dead in Christ shall rise first:

Jude (1 verses) 1:9 – "Yet Michael the archangel, when contending with the devil he disputed about the body of Moses, durst not bring against him a railing accusation, but said, The Lord rebuke thee."

The Book of Tobias (Tobit) 12:15 names Raphael as "one of the seven who stand before the Lord." Revelation 8:2 also refers to the seven angels who stand before the Lord.

Abaddon, Beelzebul, Gabriel, Michael, and Satan. Three are fallen angels and two serve God.

In Isaiah 6:1-6 "In the year that King Uzziah died I saw also the Lord sitting upon a throne, high and lifted up, and his train filled the temple. 2 Above it stood the Seraphims: each one had six wings; with twain he covered his face, and with twain he covered his feet, and with twain he did fly. 3 And one cried unto another, and said, Holy, holy, holy, is the Lord of hosts: the whole earth is full of his glory. 4 And the posts of the door moved at the voice of him that cried, and the house was filled with smoke. 5 Then said I, Woe is me! for I am undone; because I am a man of unclean lips, and I dwell in the midst of a people of unclean lips: for mine eyes have seen the King, the Lord of hosts. 6 Then flew one of the Seraphims unto me, having a live coal in his hand, which he had taken with the tongs from off the altar:"

A Seraphim is among the highest order of angels. They have three sets of wings. They are often portrayed as the winged head of a child. Our first introduction to the Seraphim was in Isaiah's vision. They use one pair of wings to hover, one pair to cover their face and one pair of wings to cover their feet. Isaiah said the Seraphims, hovering above God, were locked in perpetual song. They sung to each other, "Holy, holy, holy, is the Lord of heavenly hosts, the whole earth is filled with his glory." Their primary duty is to praise God constantly.

Most of us think of Cherubs or Cherubim as chubby babies. That is what I was thinking until I started researching. The Bible talks about them in the book of Genesis and the book of Ezekiel. They are also described in building the Ark of the Covenant. The holy part of the

Temple where the Ark of the Covenant was placed also featured statues of Cherubim. Their role is to guard God's holy domain against the presence of sin and corruption. Nowhere in the Bible is Cherubim ever referred to as angels.

The Seraphim fly above the Throne of God and the Cherubim fly around the Throne of God.

Another type of angel is the Chayot Hakodesh. These are the angels which Ezekiel saw in his vision of the Divine Chariot or Merkabah in Ezekiel Chapter 1. It describes the living creatures, each of which has four wings, each of which has four faces of a man, lion, ox, and an eagle. The word "Merkabah" is also found 44 times in the Old Testament. These are the highest of the holy angels. The Seraphims are below them and the Cherubims rank after the Seraphim and are second highest in the hierachy of angels. They were manlike in appearance and double-winged.

Messengers of God are called Malachias. They are just below the Seraphim. They appeared to Abraham, Isaac, Moses and Jacob.

Is the Satyr and Centaur a myth? Isaiah 13:21 reads as follows: "21 But wild beasts of the desert shall lie there, and their houses shall be full of doleful creatures; and owls shall dwell there, and satyrs shall dance there. "However, Centaur are not listed in the Bible.

What may be of interest but I do not know if it is true:

Archangel Sandalphon rules the Seventh Heaven and is the protector of Earth. He is known as the Angel of Mercy and Angel of Prayer. His name may mean "co-brother." He is the twin brother of Metatron. They are the only two archangels who were originally mortal men. Sandalphon was the prophet Elijah and Metatron was the prophet Enoch. http://www.esoteric-school.org/esoteric-encyclopedia/19-archangel-sandalphon.html.

The Archangels are most frequently mentioned in the Bible. That may be because they have such an exclusive role as God's messengers at critical times in history.

Haniel, also known as Anael, Hanael, Aniel meaning "Joy of God" or "Grace of God," in Judaism folklore carries a scepter, cross and sword. He/She symbolizes beauty, friendship and pleasure and is said to be able to change your mood from great sadness to happiness. He brings harmony and inspiration to all lives. He was closely associated to Lucifer before he became a fallen angel.

Raphael meaning doctor of medicine is charged with healing the earth and protecting the young, innocent and travelers. In the Book of Tobit, Raphael was sent by God to help Tobit, Tobiah and Sarah. According to the Talmud, he was one of the three angels who visited Abraham after his circumcision. In the book of Enoch, Raphael found Azazel hand and foot and cast him into the darkness, burying him under rocks in the desert.

Archangel Camael, aka Chamuel, aka Kamael, or Samael (he who sees God) is the Archangel of Divine Justice and the Gatekeeper of Heaven. He is regarded as Chief of the Order of Powers. Besides Gabriel, he is considered to be one of the Archangels that comforted Jesus at Gethsemane. Some believe he is the angel that wrestled with Jacob.

Zadkiel, aka Sachiel, aka Zedekiel, aka Zadakiel, aka Tzadakiel, aka Zedekul, aka Hesedekiel is said to be the angel that prevented Abraham from sacrificing his son Isaac. He is also said to be one of the nine rulers of Heaven and one of the seven archangels next to God. He is one of two chieftans that assist Michael when he goes to battle. He is in fourth position in the Sephirot which corresponds to Mercy.

Tzaphkiel (means to dream) is the angel of deep contemplation of God. She is considered to be the Angel of Mercy.

Archangel Raziel is the keeper of secrets and the Angel of Mysteries. He knows all the secrets of the universe and how it operates. Raziel wrote a book and gave it to Adam who passed it down. The book passed from Adam through his son and through Enoch, through Methuselah, Lamach, Noah and his sons, and then it was passed to Solomon who gained the wisdom.

Archangel Metatron is considered to be the most supreme of angelic beings. After arriving in Heaven, he transformed into a spirit of fire and was equipped with 36 pairs of wings, as well as innumerable eyes. He lives in the Seventh Heaven and when called upon appears as a pillar of fire said to be brighter than the sun. He is the Angel of Death to which God gives daily order for souls to be taken. He then delegates these orders to Gabriel and Sammael. Metatron is the teacher of prematurely deceased children who are in Paradise. He was the prophet Enoch and the twin brother of Elijah. He taught sons the art of building cities and enacting laws. He discovered the knowledge of the Zodiac and the course of the planets. He pointed out to mankind that they should worship God, fast, pray, tithe, and give alms.

http://www.esoteric-school.org/esoteric-encyclopedia/7-archangel-metatron.html

According to the Book of King Solomon, when Moses arrived at the summit of Mt. Sinai to meet with God, he was taken in a cloud to heaven and first was met by an angel named Keniel who would not allow him to pass until he gave the name of God. He then came to a second gate that was guarded by an angel named Hadarniel who would not allow him to enter until God told Hadarniel to let Moses in. Moses came to a third gate guarded by an angel named Sandalfon and God also had to order Sandalfon to allow Moses to be admitted into Heaven. Sandalfon led Moses to God's Palace where Moses went inside and stood before the veil in front of God's Throne of Glory.

At that time, another angel, Jephephiel, appeared with the Torah, opened it, and allowed Moses to copy the entire document. This took forty days.

Life after death as we know it?

IX

AUTOMATIC WRITING
PSYCHOGRAHY

Automatic writing is another instance when you should use your spirit guide. You can channel your spirit guide through writing. In automatic writing, you have to set aside your own mind and allow your spirit guide to come through or download so to speak through writing.

Others say, however, that it is not necessarily your spirit guide that you are channeling and that it could be a demon spirit, so as the Bible warns, you should not be practicing automatic writing.

Some psychics say if you are going to do automatic writing or use the Ouija Board that you should always ask the spirit if it is a good spirit before proceeding. If it responds affirmative, then it is safe to proceed. If you do not receive a response, it is not safe to proceed.

But some also say you should safeguard yourself with protective crystals, or black tourmaline, or a protective cloak such as covering yourself in white light, and beginning by saying a prayer such as

"Great Divine Spirit, I ask for your guidance and
protection at this time. May all who come forward be
of, and from the light. I ask my guardian spirit to block
all negative entities or spirits from being present in this
place. Amen."

Automatic writing is a good way to contact your spirit guides if you
want to communicate with them. It is a way to give them permission
to communicate back to you because you can be assured they will not
allow any harm come to you.

You can do simple stuff – parlor games stuff. Ask your guide what
the weather will be tomorrow. Ask him something you already know
you. When you are more comfortable, then you can allow him to do
more serious writing – give you a real message.

Some say to do automatic writing you have to be in an altered state
of consciousness. That is not true. You just do not use your conscious
mind. It is kind of like multi-tasking. You must ignore what one hand
is doing while you are doing something with the other. When you are
typing, you do not think of the letters you are typing. You just type.
In automatic writing, you are writing, but you are thinking about
something else entirely. You could be talking to someone about another
subject, or you could be reading a book or watching television. When
your hand stops, you can check out your message. You really have no
idea what your hand is writing because everything you write is all one
long word and it does not look anything like your own handwriting.

There are dangers to automatic writing. So far, we have talked about
your spirit guide - one who is there to guide and protect you for your
entire life. But after a while people tend to believe they can then branch
out to having contact with other spirits. All other spirits are not so nice.
They may come on at the beginning as benevolent spirits but in actuality
be demonic spirits.

Many are skeptical about the authenticity of automatic writing. I
might also be a skeptic if I had not experienced it myself. I might even
be a practitioner of it if I was not a religious person. It is a curious
medium between two dimensions. But if God had wanted me to

explore automatic writing he would not have told me to leave it alone. Under my circumstances, I do not believe it would have made a positive contribution to the world.

I have referred to two instances in this book where I experienced automatic writing and in the first instance I believe it was my Guardian Angel sending me a message during a very troubling period of my life. The second time, I was a fool. I knew I was safe the first time, and so I had no fear the second time. I did not call on my Guardian Angel and had I not shut down as soon as I felt the message was finished; the consequence could have been very serious.

If you Google "automatic writing," or "psychography" you can read many stories from people about their experiences with automatic writing. Some believe they are communicating with their spirit guides. Some believe they are communicating with an angel. Some believe they are actually communicating with God. And then there are those that find out that they are communicating with the devil.

This is why God was so forbidding in His warnings to the Jewish people back in the Old Testament that they were not to engage in any way, manner, or method with any kind of occult activity whatsoever!

In the mid-1800's, automatic writing became as popular as séances and trance mediums. Ordinary people accepted automatic writing as a way for mediums to receive communications from the spirit world. The communications always inspired others to communicate with famous dead spirits. Some literary spirits dictated entire books.

Automatic Writing is the ability (easily learned) to let entities from another plane of existence, to possess your hand to leave a message for you or someone else. The writer may or may not know who the spirit is that is using his hand. The spirit may be demonic and hide his true identity.

"Automatic writing is the practice of allowing a spirit to enter one's body and to communicate through writing messages with pen and paper. The process usually begins with the practitioner placing himself or herself in a meditative state and inviting a spirit, usually referred to as their "spirit guide," to either take control of their thoughts or their hand directly. Through the person, the spirit supposedly answers questions and provides insights into the future. The writing may take the form of the person, or it can take on a completely different and sometime violent form.

'The appeal of automatic writing appears to be the ability to gain knowledge from the spirit realm. The dangers should be evident to anyone who has even begun reading this article. Entering a state of meditation clears one's mind, creating a void that is filled by the demonic. Allowing a spirit to take over your mind or body is extremely dangerous, as you may or may not be able to get it to leave. Once you have made the initial invitation, there is nothing to stop the spirit from returning at will (its will, not yours).

'The Lord created our bodies to be temples for His Hold Spirit and to be used to serve and glorify Him, not to be given over to spirits for any reason.

'The mere desire to have a "spirit guide" is an offense to the Lord beyond anything you can imagine. Jesus said in Romans 8:14:

'For as many as are led by the Spirit of God, these are the sons of God.

'God's will is that we submit ourselves to His leading in every area of our lives, for He, alone, is capable of guiding us in the way that is best for us. Seeking to be led by any other spirit is to deny Christ His Rightful Lordship over your life, and denies you the blessings of His infinite knowledge and loving care for you. To give consent for a spirit to take over your mind or body is the ultimate act of foolishness." http://www.unchainedgospel.com/dangers-of-the-occult-channeling-automatic-writing

Once again, automatic writing is proof, to me, at least, of life after death. If I had not personally experienced it, I might not be writing this, but I have personally experienced automatic writing and know it to be a valid medium between this life and the after-life.

X

ATHEISTS

I read that in a Thurmont, Maryland cemetery there is a tombstone over one grave that reads "Here lies an Atheist, all dressed up and no place to go." A few days ago, someone posted a picture of that tombstone on Google Plus.

The term "atheism" originated from the Greek atheos, meaning "without god(s)," used as a pejorative term applied to those thought to reject the gods worshiped by the larger society. The first individuals to identify themselves using the word "atheist" lived in the 18th century.

Many atheists hold that atheism is a more parsimonious worldview than theism and therefore that the burden of proof lies not on the atheist to disprove the existence of God but on the theist to provide a rationale for theism (the belief that at least one deity exists). An atheist denies the existence of a god or divine beings. An agnostic believes it is impossible to know whether there is a God without sufficient evidence. An infidel is an unbeliever, especially one who does not accept Christianity or Islam; the word is usually pejorative.

A poll in 2004 showed that 7% of the world's population were atheists and a poll in 2012 showed 13%.

When an atheist called Dr. Ben Carson a moron for believing in God, Dr. Carson said, "I believe I came from God, and you believe you came from a monkey, and you've convinced me you're right."

Theodicean atheists believe that the world as they experience it cannot be reconciled with the qualities commonly ascribed to God and gods by theologians. They argue that an omniscient, omnipotent, and omnibenevolent God is not compatible with a world where there is evil and suffering, and where divine love is hidden from many people. A similar argument is attributed to Siddhartha Gautama, the founder of Buddhism. But I do not see where they take in the fact that God gave us free will, or that we don't call on Him for help at all.

Atheism is acceptable within some religious and spiritual belief systems, including Hinduism, Jainism, Buddhism, Syntheism, Raëlism, and Neopagan movements such as Wicca. Āstika schools in Hinduism hold atheism to be a valid path to moksha, but extremely difficult, for the atheist cannot expect any help from the divine on their journey. Jainism believes the universe is eternal and has no need for a creator deity, however, Tirthankaras are revered that can transcend space and time and have more power than the god Indra. Secular Buddhism does not advocate belief in gods. Early Buddhism was atheistic as Gautama Buddha's path involved no mention of gods. Later conceptions of Buddhism consider Buddha himself a god, suggest adherents can attain godhood, and revere Bodhisattvas and Eternal Buddha. https://en.wikipedia.org/wiki/Atheism

An atheist's creed goes like this:

"An Atheist loves himself and his fellow man instead of a god. An Atheist accepts that heaven is something for which we should work now – here on earth – for all men together to enjoy. An atheist accepts that he can get no help through prayer, but that he must find in himself the inner conviction and strength to meet life, to grapple with it, to subdue it and to enjoy it. An atheist accepts that only in a knowledge of himself and a knowledge of his fellow man can he find the understanding that will help lead to a life of fulfillment." http://atheists.org/about-us

Atheism is the absence of belief in any god. Someone who denies the existence of God.

Agnosticism is not about belief in God, but about knowledge – it was coined originally to describe the position of a person who could not claim to know for sure if any gods exist or not. You can claim to believe in God without claiming to know for sure God exists (agnostic theism). Or, you can disbelieve in God without claiming to know for sure that God exists (agnostic atheism). http://atheism.about.com/od/aboutagnosticism/a/atheism.htm

Some things an atheist cannot do are:

1. Atheists in 13 countries face execution under the law if they openly express their beliefs or reject the official state religion — Islam in all of these cases.
2. Despite constitutional restrictions on "religious tests" for holding public office, six states have laws on the books barring nonbelievers, not to mention placing your hand on a Bible for being sworn into office.
3. Atheists have trouble being trusted even when they're not running for office. A survey taken in 2012 found that half of Americans believed atheism was "threatening" to them. Another study by the University of British Columbia and the University of Oregon found that people are likely to distrust atheists as much as they do rapists.
4. During his swearing-in speech in 2011, Alabama Gov. Robert Bentley (R) threw inclusiveness out the window when he made these comments about religion:
4. "So anybody here today who has not accepted Jesus Christ as their savior, I'm telling you, you're not my brother and you're not my sister, and I want to be your brother," he said. It's hard to imagine any other class of people, especially one so large — we're not just talking nonbelievers here, but people of all non-Christian faiths — being so casually and expressly dismissed.

5. Nonbelievers also have faced discrimination after being hired. In 2010, a math teacher was fired from her position at a Catholic school after someone noticed she'd joined an atheist website from her home computer and made comments on Facebook about not believing in God. A few years' prior, a government and history teacher in Texas was allegedly fired simply over the suspicion that he was an atheist.

6. If atheists can't be trusted to be good employees, they certainly can't be trusted to be responsible parents. Over the past few decades, there have been many documented cases of judges either denying parents' custody rights because of their apparent disinterest in organized religion or in other cases, of atheist parents being ordered to attend church so that their children can undergo "systematic spiritual training."

7. When the Upstate Atheists, a charity organization in Spartanburg, S.C., offered to lend a hand volunteering at a local soup kitchen last year, they were surprised to hear that the director of the facility would have rather resigned than work alongside godless members of the community. While the atheists said they had no plans to bring religion into the mix at all, the soup kitchen's director complained that they were "targeting" her organization. The Upstate Atheists responded by setting up shop across the street from the soup kitchen and handing out 300 care packages to homeless people.

8. The Boy Scouts of America still prohibits atheists from joining its ranks.
   http://www.huffingtonpost.com/2014/01/16/atheists-discrimination_n_4413593.html

Atheists are apparently so detestable that a group of military veteran nonbelievers was repeatedly heckled and berated in 2011 during a Memorial Day parade. Apparently supporting the troops comes with a big asterisk, which maybe isn't a shock, considering the military's own record of discriminating against service members who don't believe in God.

XI

THE MISSING BOOKS OF
THE BIBLE

There are many "missing" books of the Bible. For instance, there were fifteen books that were part of the Apocrypha, a part of the Greek translation of the Bible, but not accepted by Protestants because they were not part of the original Hebrew Scriptures. The Bible is a collection written over many centuries by many different people and eventually accepted by Jews and later Christians as Holy Scriptures. The term Apocrypha means "questionable authenticity." They were called non-canonical books because when the original sixty-six books were incorporated into the Bible, these books were considered to be "not inspired by God.

However, the Roman Catholic Church declared that certain writings from the Apocrypha were inspired, and they were included in the Catholic Bible. Those books are Tobit, Judith, Wisdom of Solomon, Ecclesiasticus, Baruch, 1 & 2 Maccabees, Letter of Jeremiah, additions to Esther, Prayer of Azariah, Susanna (Daniel 13), Bel and the Dragon (Daniel 14). Three other books, Prayer of Manasseh, and 1 & 2 Esdras are not considered to be inspired or canonical by the Roman Catholic Church.

Sometime after the death of Jesus when Christianity became a religion separate from Judaism, leaders of the new church compiled their own Holy Scriptures designated as the Septuagint version of the Bible, including the additions as the Old Testament. The Message of Jesus, The Savior, and the writings of his followers became known as the New Testament and became today's Christian Bible.

Basically, there were four reasons the Apocrypha were not included in the Old and New Testament Bible. 1) They have many historical and geographical inaccuracies; 2) They teach false doctrines and encourage practices which are in conflict with inspired scriptures; 3) They display subject matter, not in keeping with inspired scriptures; and 4) They lack the distinctive elements which give genuine scriptures their divine character, such as prophetic feeling.

Although the Apocrypha existed before New Testament times, there is no single quotation quoted by Jesus or any of his Apostles from any book of the Apocrypha. Jesus quotes from 24 books of the Old Testament and the New Testament quotes from 34 books of the Old Testament. The Apocrypha were originally included in the Bible in the King James Bible and were positioned between the Old and New Testament. They remained there for 274 years, or until 1885 A.D.

The Jews did not include the Apocrypha because they believe the material is heretical and contains gross doctrinal errors; one of which praying for the dead. (2 Macc. 12:45-46 – And also in that they perceived that there was great favour laid up for those that died godly, it was a holy and good thought. After that they made reconciliation for the dead, that they might be delivered from sin.) and salvation by works. (Tobit 12:9 For alms doth deliver from death and shall purge away all sin. Those that exercise alms and righteousness shall be filled with life.). Praying for the dead is not biblical as Hebrews 9:27 plainly states, "And as it is appointed unto men once to die, but after this the judgment." There is no second chance after death. Ephesians 2:8-9 clearly states that salvation is not by works or merited by man. "For by grace are ye saved through faith; and that not of yourselves: it is the gift of God: Not of works, lest any man should boast."

"In the Fourth Century, a Christian Scholar named Jerome was given the task of translating the Bible into Latin. In his translation, called the Vulgate, Jerome included those books of the old Testament which appeared in the Septuagint, but not in the Hebrew Bible, as well as a few others. He proposed to call these additional books Apocrypha.

'Although this title is widely used, it frequently caused misunderstanding. At one time, Apocrypha was a term used to describe books that were "hidden away" because they were considered too esoteric or sacred for the common reader. Later, Apocrypha described heretical Christian works, and came to mean "questionable" or "not trustworthy." The case of the additional books of the Septuagint is different, however." [The Missing Books of the Bible]

Most of the Apocryphal books remain in Roman Catholic Bibles. The Old Testament and Apocrypha biblical characters are called by slightly different names. For example; Ezra/Esdras. Jeremiah/Jeremy.

The First Volume of the Missing Books of the Bible contains the following books: The First Book of Esdras; The Second Book of Esdras; The Book of Tobit; The Book of Judith; The Rest of the Chapters of the Book of Esther; and the Wisdom of Solomon.

Volume Two of the Missing Books of the Bible contains the following books: The Wisdom of Jesus, The Son of Sirach; The Book of Baruch; The Epistle of Jeremy; The Prayer of Azariah; The History of Susanna; The History of the Destruction of Bel and The Dragon; The Prayer of Manasses; The First Book of Maccabees; and The Second Book of Maccabees.

The New Testament did not emerge as a complete set of books after the death of Jesus. Many years had passed before Christians agreed which books should comprise the sacred scriptures. Even at that time, there were other books available, but they advocated different points of view than those presently embodied by the Bible. These differences were not minor issues and if included in the Bible, would change Christianity as we know it today.

When the New Testament was being put together, for instance, seventeen non-canonical gospels were rejected; five non-canonical Acts of the Apostles were rejected; thirteen non-canonical epistles and related writings were rejected; seven non-canonical Apocalypses and Revelatory Treatises were rejected, and Five Canonical Lists were rejected.

It would be easy to understand why these books were rejected as they deal with the spirit world. In the Gospel of Mary (Magdalene), Peter said to Mary --

"Sister, we know that the Savior loved you more than the rest of the women. Tell us the words of the Savior, which you remember—which you know (but) we do not, nor have we heard them."

Mary answered and said, "What is hidden from you I will proclaim to you." And she began to speak to them these words: "I," she said, "I saw the Lord in a vision, and I said to him, 'Lord, I saw you today in a vision.'

He answered and said to me, 'Blessed are you that you did not waver at the sight of me. For where the mind is, there is the treasure.'

I said to him, 'Lord how does he who sees the vision see it <through> the soul <or> through the spirit?'

The Savior answered and said, "He does not see through the soul nor through the spirit, but the mind which [is] between the two – that is [what] sees the vision [....] p.11-14 missing].

[....] it. And desire that. 'I did not see you descending, but now I see you ascending.

Why do you lie since you belong to me?' The soul answered and said, 'I saw you. You did not see me, nor recognize me. I served you as a garment, and you did not know me.' When it had said this, it went away rejoicing greatly.

"Again it came to the third power which is called ignorance. It (the power) questioned the soul saying, "Where are you going? In wickedness are you bound? But you are bound; Do not judge!" And the soul said, why do you judge me although I have not judged? I was bound although I have not bound. I was not recognized. But I have recognized that the All is being dissolved, both the earthly (things) and the heavenly."

"When the soul had overcome the third power, it went upwards and saw the fourth power. (which) took seven forms. The first form is darkness, the second desire, the third ignorance, the fourth is the excitement of death, the fifth is the kingdom of the flesh, the sixth is the foolish wisdom of the flesh, and the seventh is the wrathful wisdom. These are the seven powers of wrath......"

Can you imagine how mankind would interpret just this one book if it were in the New Testament? This connection with Gnosticism, together with the prominent role that the book gives to a female, may have led to its suppression by orthodox Christians.

One of the books is The Gospel of Truth. I have read it several times, and it is so complex, and far out I still do not know what it says.

During the Nineteenth Century, a fragment of the Gospel of Peter was found in Egypt. It is hopeful that more will someday be found as the fragment indicates that Peter was present at the time Jesus came out of the tomb with two angels just before he ascended into Heaven.

The Gospel of Thomas indicates that it contains "secret sayings" of Jesus and gives 114 of these sayings. Jesus speaks as a teacher, and the disciples ask questions and comment. Some scholars believed it contained secret knowledge.

A damaged copy of the Gospel of Judas was found on the black market in Egypt. Some pages are missing, but the manuscript may indicate that Judas was the most loyal disciple of Jesus and was innocent instead of an evil betrayer.

The Lost Q Source also known as The Lost Sayings Gospel and the Q Document thought to be the source of many of original sources of Jesus' teachings. Some say they are nothing more than a collection from early Christian missionaries as an aid in spreading the new faith.

Pre-Markan Narrative - Scholars have deduced the probable existence of this gospel from careful studies of the Gospel of Mark. These studies indicate that the author of Mark obtained some material from an earlier source. This source has been lost, but the evidence indicates that it was a short narrative of the arrest, interrogation, and crucifixion of Jesus. For this reason, it is called the Pre-Markan Passion Narrative.

The unknown author of this lost narrative had a good knowledge of what happened to Jesus during and after his arrest. The narrative might have even been written by a member of the first community of believers, known as the Nazarenes, who lived in Jerusalem in the years after Jesus departed.

Reconstructions of the original form of this book indicate that it gave a simple straight-forward account of what happened before and after the crucifixion. Because this account may be the basis for all the later accounts, whoever wrote it performed an extremely important service.

http://www.archive.org/stream/LostBooksOfTheBible/Lost BooksOfTheBible_djvu.txt

The Signs Gospel – known as The Gospel of John because it describes some miracles of Jesus known as signs. These signs that Jesus was the Messiah included his changing the water into wine, giving sight to the man that was born blind, healing the man at the Pool of Bethesda, and the raising of Lazarus from the dead.

The First and Second Book of Adam and Eve is a book from the time Adam and Eve were thrown out of the Garden of Eden when they got married, their having five children, not three, and up through the time, Enoch was transported to Heaven by God.

The Gospel of the Savior was found in Egypt and remained unnoticed until 1991 when two scholars published the first edition of the text. It was difficult because the manuscript was full of holes. The author is unknown, and the original language was in Greek.

In Verses 28-36, A vision on the Mount, the author says: "28. [... 12+ lines untranslatable...] on the mountains. 29. We became spiritual bodies. Our eyes opened wide in every direction. The whole place was revealed before us. 30. We [saw] the heavens, and they [opened] up one after another. 31. The guardians of the gates were alarmed. 32. The angels were afraid and [fled] this [way] and that, thinking [that] they would all be destroyed. 3. We saw our Savior having penetrated all the heavens, [his] feet [placed firmly on] the [mountain with us, his head, penetrating the seventh] heaven. 34. [... 8 lines untranslatable---] all the heavens. 35. Then before us, the apostles, this world became as darkness. 36. We became as [those] among the [immortal] aeons, with our [eyes penetrating all] the heavens, clothed with the [power of] our apostleship, and we saw our Savior when he had reached the [seventh] heaven."

These are only a few examples of the verses that lean towards the outer edge. A reading of some of the other books would take someone far more enlightened than I to understand.

Had all the lost books been included in the Bible, instead of Christians, we would have a world of spiritualists.

It also points to a world of many dimensions or many levels of heaven. How many dimensions we do not know. Many people have many different opinions. Here is a simple explanation that is uncomplicated.

"The Third Dimension – Our Physical Reality of the Conscious Being

'This is the plane of thought or mind, the illusion of free will. We cannot detect the spirit which is beyond form. "If we are not at one with the Spirit, then we cannot be at one with others."

'The Third Dimension is the material world. It is where we need to control our space, where we need to mate, where we need to rule, where we need to create our own reality.

'The Fourth Dimension – The Astral Plane

'This plane is that of Will or Life-spirit and it is of this dimension that the individual "self," the Ego, is a part. It is the Ego who uses the physical, astral and mind bodies as tools with which to achieve its purpose. When mind, body, and spirit are completely aligned with Divine Will and in harmony and balance... one with another... you are omnipotent and have achieved conquest over matter.

'When a person astral travels, this is the plane he goes. When Edgar Cayce read from the Akashic Records, this is where he traveled.

'The Fifth Dimension – Heaven – The Plane of Light

'The highest realm a soul can reach. There is no physical suffering. Since there is no form of separation, we constantly experience the Oneness of Father Creator. We base our actions entirely on love, never fear. Fear does not exist on this level." http://www.bibliotecapleyades. net/ciencia/ciencia_dimensionshyperdimensions02.htm

XII

OUR BODIES

Some say you only live once, but that is wrong. You live every day. You only die once, and everyone owes a death. Death, as we know it, is certain.

"It is his soul that goes to Heaven or Hell, whichever the case may be. Our bodies are nothing more than housing for our souls. These bodies are not what go with us when we die. When our souls return to God, we are given perfect, heavenly bodies that, to my understanding, do not look like what we are in now, although we will know one another.

'We know from the scriptures that only our soul goes on to Heaven or Hell, not our body. Does it go directly to Heaven for judgment or does it wait somewhere for the second coming of Jesus and the Judgment to follow? The puzzle is that we are dealing with an unanswerable question at the human level.

'The Christian religion is the only one that has the offer of a life after death because of the sacrifice of one person. If there is no Christ and no Crucifixion and no Resurrection, then there is no Christian religion.

'If there is only death and nothing beyond, there is no need for a Soul.

'We tend to apply human thinking to the resting place of our soul. We talk about riding on clouds and playing on heavenly harps and other human imaginings. Paradise is most likely a place without time or space limits, and without pain or other human sensations.

'Since there is no time or space how can the time or the place of judgment even be determined. It can't. A decision made as to the destination of the Soul could be made in the first nanosecond or in thousands of years because there is no awareness of time. This is why the Bible refers to a day is as a thousand years to God."

http://www.fullerbiblestudy.com/Where_does_my_Soul_go_when_I_die/

Where does the mind go for those that are in a coma? Are you in between life and death? Life means the state of living, thinking and acting. A person in a coma can respond to stimuli, but where does the mind go? Usually, a person eventually revives but they do not remember any part of the time they were in the coma. Everything is blank to them.

"Scientists still don't understand exactly how human consciousness works, but the twilight state of a coma could reveal some insight. Past research revealed that a person in a coma is closer to being anesthetized than being asleep. Other studies have found that vegetative and minimally conscious patients have very different brain activity.

'But for the most part, it was hard to find obvious differences in brain functioning between healthy patients and those who have lost consciousness.

'To tease out these differences, Achard [Sophie Achard, a statistician at the French National Center for Scientific Research in Grenoble] and her colleagues took functional magnetic resonance imaging (MRI) brain scans of 17 patients who were in a coma a few days after cardiac arrest and compared them with scans from 20 healthy volunteers who were at rest. Some patients, who had lost oxygen to the brain for up to 30 to 40 minutes, eventually recovered, but more than half died.

'The team tracked 417 different brain regions for changes in blood flow — a marker of brain activity. They then correlated synchronized increases or decreases in activity between different regions.

'In healthy patients, about 40 regions lit up in concert with many other parts of the brain. These high-traffic hubs, like busy airports, apparently process much of the electrical firing in the brain.

'But in the coma patients, many of these hubs were darkened, and other, normally peripheral regions took their place. Intriguingly, coma patients had fewer hubs in a region called the precuneus, which is known to play a role in consciousness and memory.

'These central nodes of brain activity may hold the key to consciousness, Achard told LiveScience. Because they direct so much of the brain's traffic, they also require more oxygen and thus may be more vulnerable to its loss.... http://www.foxnews.com/health/2012/11/27/what-happens-to-brain-in-coma.html

You are born into this world for a specific purpose that is just your purpose, and your purpose alone. It does not matter how long you are in this world. When that purpose has been fulfilled, your time here expires. It can be one day, or it can be many years.

Death is simply shedding our bodies for a higher state of consciousness where we continue to laugh and thrive. The only thing you lose is your physical body. Out of all of the research done on Near Death Experiences and Out-of-Body Experiences, not one of the people interviewed expressed a fear of dying again or leaving their body again on a permanent basis. To the contrary, they expressed not looking forward to returning to their body and the continuation of living.

The biggest fear we all have is dying alone. No one wants to die and not have our bodies found until several days or weeks later.

Of course, there are those that believe you die, and that is the end, that there is nothing else.

Atheists believe you die and that is the end; that you just take a dirt nap when you pass on. But according to the thousands of people that gave information on their near-death-experiences, not one of them was alone at the time of death. Always your guides, your guardian angels, the people you have loved that have previously passed, are there to greet you when you die. The people you see are the people that you have loved the most in this lifetime. It could be a spouse, your parents, a deceased child, or a sibling.

When a husband and wife die, in the next life they are no longer husband and wife. That does not mean that a husband and wife will not know each other in heaven or have a close relationship in heaven. It is just that no one is married in heaven. God created marriage as a means of procreation and colonizing the earth with human beings. Heaven, however, does not need to be populated by procreation. The people that go to heaven will get there by faith in the Lord Jesus Christ; they will not get there by means of reproduction. Therefore, there is no purpose for marriage in heaven since there is no reproduction or loneliness – only love.

Matthew 22:30 says: "In the resurrection they neither marry nor are given in marriage..."

The Bible refers to dying as sleeping and sleeping may be a better word than dying since you are simply moving from one house (your body) to a more beautiful home. In this first stage, you are supplied with "physical energy." When you leave your body and enter the second stage, you are supplied with psychic energy because you still need a functioning brain and consciousness to communicate. Physical and Psychic Energies are the only two energies that man can manipulate.

If you approach the bed of a dying family member, it does not matter whether you think they can hear you or not, even if they are in a coma. It is never too late to say "I am sorry" or "I love you," or whatever else you want to say because they can still hear you. There are many reports that says a person in a coma can hear you.

You have probably heard many people use the expression "well, he doesn't have to suffer anymore," and regardless of why they said, or how they said it, it is true.

When you are in Stage Two and have become psychic energy, you are in a life or presence, or existence where time no longer exists. This is why a deceased or out-of-body person can travel miles in seconds by a thought to see anyone he wants.

After you realize that your body is perfect and whole again and without pain and that you have met your loved ones again, you realize that death is just a transition to a different form of life. It is at this time that many describe going through a tunnel, or perhaps crossing a bridge, where at the end is the light that is whiter than white. The closer you get to the light the more you are enfolded by unconditional love.

For those interviewed by researchers that have had Near Death Experiences or Out-of-Body Experiences that went so far as to see the light, very few of them wanted to come back to their bodies. Most of them said they felt such love that they did not want to return. Here is where you find out that in your life here on earth you were just being educated and now is the time to get your diploma.

XIII

JUDGMENT DAY AND THE SOUL OF MAN

Born-again Christians believe that they will stand before Jesus Christ to give an account for their lives immediately following the rapture. One of the reasons for this is found in 2 Corinthians 5:10 where it states: "For we must all appear before the judgment seat of Christ, so that each of us may receive what is due us for the things done while in the body, whether good or bad" (NIV).

According to the Christian Bible, in Revelation 20:11- "And I saw a great white throne, and Him that sat on it, from whose face the earth and the heaven fled away; and there was found no place for them. 12 And I saw the dead, small and great, stand before God; and the books were opened: and another book was opened, which is the book of life: and the dead were judged out of those things which were written in the books, according to their works. 13 And the sea gave up the dead which were in it; and death and hell delivered up the dead which were in them: and they were judged every man according to their works. 14 And death and hell were cast into the lake of fire. This is the second death. 15 And whosoever was not found written in the book of life was cast into the lake of fire."

"The Bible ceaselessly speaks about the soul of man. We have to understand what the soul consists of. The soul is made up of the mind, will, and emotions. It is the soul that goes to Heaven or Hell, not the body. We will not look the same in Heaven. Man does not have a soul. He is the soul. His body formed by God from the dust and the breath of life from God breathed into his nostrils created a living soul. Hence when a person dies, the body is separated from the breath of life. The body returns to the ground, and the breath of life returns to God, who gave it to man. All animals are living souls as well until they too die. Their bodies return to dust as well, and their breath of life returns to God."

http://www.answers2prayer.org/bible_questions/Answers/death/go.html

The soul is conscious after death: Rev 6:9-11 "When he opened the fifth seal, I saw under the altar the souls of those who had been slain because of the word of God and the testimony they had maintained. They called out in a loud voice, "How long, Sovereign Lord, holy and true until you judge the inhabitants of the earth and avenge our blood?" Then each of them was given a white robe, and they were told to wait a little longer until the number of their fellow servants and brothers who were to be killed as they had been was completed." NIV

Man's spirit is what is born again: John 3:6-7 "Flesh gives birth to flesh, but the Spirit gives birth to spirit. You should not be surprised at my saying, 'You must be born again.'" NIV

Proverbs 20:27 "The lamp of the Lord searches the spirit of a man; it searches out his inmost being." NIV

Man's Spirit has intelligence: 1 Cor. 2:11 "For who among men knows the thoughts of a man except the man's spirit within him? In the same way, no one knows the thoughts of God except the Spirit of God." NIV

The soul and the spirit are separated from the body at death: Luke 8:54-56 "But he took her by the hand and said, "My child, get up!" 55 Her spirit returned, and at once she stood up. Then Jesus told them to give her something to eat." NIV

Matt 10:28 "Do not be afraid of those who kill the body but cannot kill the soul. Rather, be afraid of the One, who can destroy both soul and body in hell." NIV

James 2:26 "As the body without the spirit is dead, so faith without deeds is dead." NIV

1 Kings 17:21-23 "Then he stretched himself out on the boy three times and cried to the Lord, "O Lord my God, let this boy's life return to him!" The Lord heard Elijah's cry, and the boy's life returned to him, and he lived." NIV

Many scriptures state that when you die the body sleeps. For instance, in the story of Lazarus and the story of Stephen, the scripture refers to both of them as sleeping, not as being dead, although in our vernacular today we would refer to them as being dead. Is it possible the term was used because it looked like the person was sleeping? When Stephen was being stoned, he prayed, "Lord Jesus, receive my spirit."

Psalms 6:5 says: "For in death there is no remembrance of thee: in the grave who shall give thee thanks?"

And in Ecclesiastes 9:5-10 it says: "For the living know that they shall die: but the dead know not anything, neither have they any more a reward; for the memory of them is forgotten. 6 Also their love, and their hatred, and their envy, is now perished; neither have they any more a portion forever in anything that is done under the sun. 7 Go thy way, eat thy bread with joy, and drink thy wine with a merry heart; for God now accepteth thy works. 8 Let thy garments be always white, and let thy head lack no ointment. 9 Live joyfully with the wife whom thou lovest all the days of the life of thy vanity, which he hath given thee under the sun, all the days of thy vanity: for that is thy portion in this life, and in thy labour which thou takest under the sun. 10 Whatsoever thy hand findeth to do, do it with thy might; for there is no work, nor device, nor knowledge, nor wisdom, in the grave, whither thou goest."

"These passages support the argument of soul sleep, however, only if they are referring to the soul as well as the body. It is probable, however, that the verses are speaking of the fate of the body only. In discussing the meaning of the Hebrew word "Sheol," which occurs in both Psalm 6:5 and Eccl 9, R. Laird Harris writes, If this interpretation of Sheol is correct [that it means "grave" where the body is placed], its usage does not give us a picture of the state of the dead in gloom, darkness, chaos, or silence, unremembered, unable to praise God, knowing nothing. Such a view verges on unscriptural soul sleep. Rather, this view gives us a picture of a typical Palestinian tomb, dark, dusty, with mingled bones and where "this poor lisping stammering tongue lies silent in the grave."

"All the souls of men do not go to one place. But all people go to the grave. As to the destiny of the souls of men in the intermediate state, the OT [Old Testament] says little. Actually, the NT [New Testament] says little too, but what it says is decisive... (R. L. Harris, Theological Wordbook of the Old Testament, Vol. 2 (Chicago: The Moody Bible Institute, 1980) 893.)"

'The soul sleep argument is that at death the soul remains with the body and both sleep. This is flatly contradicted, however, by many places in the New Testament.

'Believers are judged at the Judgment Seat of Christ (Romans 14:10-12). Every believer will give an account of himself, and the Lord will judge the decisions he made—including those concerning issues of conscience. This judgment does not determine salvation, which is by faith alone (Ephesians 2:8-9), but rather is the time when believers must give an account of their lives in service to Christ. Our position in Christ is the "foundation" spoken of in 1 Corinthians 3:11-15. That which we build upon the foundation can be the "gold, silver, and precious stones" of good works in Christ's name, obedience, and fruitfulness—dedicated spiritual service to glorify God and build the church. Or what we build on the foundation may be the "wood, hay and stubble" of worthless, frivolous, shallow activity with no spiritual value. The Judgment Seat of Christ will reveal this.

'The gold, silver and precious stones in the lives of believers will survive God's refining fire (v. 13), and believers will be rewarded based on those good works—how faithfully we served Christ (1 Corinthians 9:4-27), how well we obeyed the Great Commission (Matthew 28:18-20), how victorious we were over sin (Romans 6:1-4), how well we controlled our tongues (James 3:1-9), etc. We will have to give an account for our actions, whether they were truly indicative of our position in Christ. The fire of God's judgment will completely burn up the "wood, hay and stubble" of the words we spoke and things we did which had no eternal value. "So then, each of us will give an account of himself to God" (Romans 14:12).

'The second judgment is that of unbelievers who will be judged at the Great White Throne Judgment (Revelation 20:11-15). This judgment does not determine salvation, either. Everyone at the Great White Throne is an unbeliever who has rejected Christ in life and is therefore already doomed to the lake of fire. Revelation 20:12 says that unbelievers will be "judged out of those things which were written in the books, according to their works." Those who have rejected Christ as Lord and Savior will be judged based on their works alone and because the Bible tells us that "by the works of the Law no flesh will be justified" (Galatians 2:16), they will be condemned. No amount of good works and the keeping of God's laws can be sufficient to atone for sin. All their thoughts, words and actions will be judged against God's perfect standard and found wanting. There will be no reward for them, only eternal condemnation and punishment." http://www.gotquestions.org/judgment.html

The Bible sets forth that everyone will be judged according to how they have lived their lives while on earth. Some Christians disagree with that because they believe God has forgiven them of their sins. Is that enough? We were put here on earth to live our life for God, not to live our life for ourselves. But we were given free will and the ability to make that choice. Romans 14:10 says "we shall all stand before the Judgment Seat of Christ."

How many preachers preach a sermon on this topic and what it really means? It is not God that will judge us. It is Jesus Christ that will judge us. You know, the one that was crucified on the cross. The one with the nail scars in his hands, not in his wrists as scientists attempt to portray. The one that arose on the third day from the grave.

Revelation 21:27 says: "And there shall in no wise enter into it anything that defileth, neither whatsoever worketh abomination, or maketh a lie: but they which are written in the Lamb's book of life." Revelation 22:19 says: "And if any man shall take away from the words of the book of this prophecy, God shall take away his part out of the book of life, and out of the holy city, and from the things which are written in this book."

This book is also the reference to be used for judgment. If a person's name is not written in this book, that person will be thrown into the lake of fire. Revelation 20:15 says: "And whosoever was not found written in the book of life was cast into the lake of fire." In short, past sins are forgiven to those who have quit sin, i.e., those for whom sinning has become a thing of the past. These are the ones who have overcome sins. These are the ones who enter the kingdom of heaven.

Christians think that salvation is an opportunity to receive an 'acquittal' verdict at the judgment of God. Contrary to this belief, there is no 'acquittal' verdict. Jesus Christ states that as long as a person is in sin, he/she is a slave to sin and is not saved: this person will face eternal death. Salvation is an escape from committing sins. A person who has escaped sin will perform the works of righteousness. Heaven and the glory thereof are given as the rewards for works of righteousness. Those who are unrighteous will receive the reward of the lake of fire.

As people are saved from their sins, they become people who do the works of righteousness. Romans 6:18 says: "Being then made free from sin, ye became the servants of righteousness." These righteous people will be rewarded for their righteous works. This reward is heaven and the glory which will be given them in heaven. Unsaved people, on the other hand, will have their part in the lake of fire. Revelation 21 says: "7) He that overcometh shall inherit all things; and I will be his God, and he shall be my son. 8) But the fearful, and unbelieving, and the abominable, and murderers, and whoremongers, and sorcerers, and idolaters, and all liars, shall have their part in the lake which burneth with fire and brimstone: which is the second death." Revelation 22:12 says: "And, behold, I come quickly; and my reward is with me, to give every man according as his work shall be." The judgment will be a reward ceremony to righteous people for their righteous works; it will be a punishment ceremony for all others for their unrighteous works. http://www.abideinchrist.info/judgment.html

XIV

WHERE DOES YOUR SOUL GO?

I think the only way to know the truth for sure is to check the Bible. In Genesis 2:7 it says, "And the Lord God formed man of the dust of the ground and breathed into his nostrils the breath of life, and man became a living soul."

At death, everything goes into reverse. In Ecclesiastes 12:7 it says, "Then shall the dust return to the earth as it was: and the spirit shall return unto God who gave it. There are two different entities that make up a human being; the body and the spirit. Each takes a different path. One goes to the ground, and the other goes to God."

The Bible tells us that our body is the house in which our spirit lives.

2 Cor. 5:2-4 "Meanwhile we groan, longing to be clothed with our heavenly dwelling because when we are clothed, we will not be found naked. For while we are in this tent, we groan and are burdened, because we do not wish to be unclothed but to be clothed with our heavenly dwelling so that what is mortal may be swallowed up by life." NIV

2 Peter 1:13 "I think it is right to refresh your memory as long as I live in the tent of this body" NIV

Our body is just the dwelling place of our spirit. Just like people's houses are just temporary places to live in, and after a while they may move to another dwelling, so is the case with our bodies. On earth, it is our dwelling. When we die we leave that dwelling behind and move on to our "heavenly dwelling."

What happens when we die then? Very simple, our bodies return to dust, while our spirit goes to be with the Lord. The apostle Paul tells us that he (2 Cor. 5:8-9) "would prefer to be away from the body and at home with the Lord." NIV

Ezekiel tells us who owns your soul and which ones will suffer destruction: Ezekiel 18:44 "For every living soul belongs to me, the father, as well as the son-both alike, belong to me. The soul who sins is the one who will die." NIV

It is not the soul that sleeps when we die; it is the body! It is not the soul or spirit that decays and returns to dust; it is the body! Our spirit returns to God. Jesus Himself made sure we knew this fact when he uttered His last words on the cross: Luke 23:46 "Father, into your hands I commit my spirit." When He had said this, He breathed His last. NIV http://www.answers2prayer.org/saviours_call.html

When you go to Church, your Minister will tell you that when you die that if you are saved your spirit will immediately go to heaven. However, Revelations 11-15 states: And I saw a great white throne, and him that sat on it, from whose face the earth and the heaven fled away; and there was found no place for them. 12 And I saw the dead, small and great, stand before God; and the books were opened: and another book was opened, which is the book of life: and the dead were judged out of those things which were written in the books, according to their works. 13 And the sea gave up the dead which were in it, and death and hell delivered up the dead which were in them: and they were judged every man according to their works. 14 And death and hell were cast into the lake of fire. This is the second death. 15 And whosoever was not found written in the book of life was cast into the lake of fire.

This would suggest that when you die that your spirit goes someplace else, another dimension, until Judgment Day.

Yet, Jesus told the thief on the cross "today, you will be with Me in paradise. That sounds like a promise that the soul would go to be with Jesus whether it be a holding place or directly to heaven. Of course, this would be the soul of the believer. The soul of the unbeliever would enter eternal hell. But you must also note that Jesus said he would be with him in "paradise," not in "heaven." Is "Paradise" the name of the intermediate holding place for souls waiting for judgment day?

As further evidence that Paradise is not Heaven, in Acts 2:29-35 the Bible states: 29 "Men and brethren, let me freely speak unto you of the patriarch David, that he is both dead and buried, and his sepulcher is with us unto this day. 30 Therefore being a prophet, and knowing that God had sworn with an oath to him, that of the fruit of his loins, according to the flesh, he would raise up Christ to sit on his throne; 31 He seeing this before spake of the resurrection of Christ, that his soul was not left in hell, neither his flesh did see corruption. 32 This Jesus hath God raised up, whereof we all are witnesses. 33 Therefore being by the right hand of God exalted and having received of the Father the promise of the Holy Ghost, he hath shed forth this, which ye now see and hear. 34 For David is not ascended into the heavens: but he saith himself, The LORD said unto my Lord, Sit thou on my right hand, 35 Until I make thy foes thy footstool."

In James 5:19-20, it was said: "Brethren, if any of you do err from the truth, and one convert him; 20 Let him know, that he which converteth the sinner from the error of his way shall save a soul from death and shall hide a multitude of sins."

And the Bible says you can lose your soul. In Mark 8:36-37 the Bible says: For what shall it profit a man if he shall gain the whole world, and lose his own soul? 37 Or what shall a man give in exchange for his soul?

And Matthew 10:28 says: And fear not them which kill the body but are not able to kill the soul: but rather fear him which is able to destroy both soul and body in hell.

Jesus told the thief on the cross "today, you will be with Me in paradise." The Seven Day Adventists' believe the punctuation was wrong on this particular scripture and that it was meant as: "Truly I say to you today, you will be with me in Paradise." But Jesus did not talk in that manner.

We know that Jesus ascended into Heaven on that day. It was his rightful place. But on his way, he also took all of the souls into heaven that had gone on before him such as Adam, Noah, Abraham, Samuel, etc. Where were these souls being held before that time? Which dimension?

Another important example of life after death and where does your soul go is the appearance of Moses on the Mount of Transfiguration. The Bible specifically states that Moses died and was buried in a valley in Moab opposite Beth Peor (Deut 34:5 "So Moses the servant of the Lord died there in the land of Moab, according to the word of the Lord. 6 And he buried him in a valley in the land of Moab, over against Bethpeor: but no man knoweth of his sepulchre unto this day.)" Yet, when Jesus was transfigured almost 1500 years later, Moses appeared "in glory" and was talking to Jesus. This is described in Luke 9:29 "And as he prayed, the fashion of his countenance was altered, and his raiment was white and glistering. 30 And, behold, there talked with him two men, which were Moses and Elias: 31 Who appeared in glory, and spake of his decease which he should accomplish at Jerusalem."

Elijah's appearance "doesn't count" because Scripture records that he did not die but was taken directly to heaven in a whirlwind (2 Kings 2:11 "And it came to pass, as they still went on and talked, that, behold, there appeared a chariot of fire, and horses of fire, and parted them both asunder; and Elijah went up by a whirlwind into heaven.")

Moses did die, however, and his body was buried. Yet he stands there in some form (spiritual or otherwise), talking to Jesus, long before the resurrection on the Last Day. Either Moses' body was raised early (of which we have no mention in Scripture – Jude 1:9 "Yet Michael the archangel, when contending with the devil he disputed about the body of Moses, durst not bring against him a railing accusation, but said, The Lord rebuke thee." is not conclusive) or his soul appeared in visible form on the Mount of Transfiguration.

Then we have the scripture in Revelation that most do not want to take literally as the rest. There John sees a vision of the souls of martyred Christians under the altar in heaven. "When he opened the fifth seal, I saw under the altar the souls of those who had been slain for the word of God and for the witness they had borne. "10 They cried out with a loud voice, O Sovereign Lord, holy and true, how long before you will judge and avenge our blood on those who dwell on the earth? 11 Then they were each given a white robe and told to rest a little longer until the number of their fellow servants and their brothers should be complete, who were to be killed as they themselves had been" (Rev 6:9-11). If this vision is to be understood literally, it is a clear example of the souls of Christians in heaven before the final Judgment. However, it is being interpreted as symbolic and said not be taken literally by some ministers."

Some say the Bible is clear in that when a person dies their soul and body both sleep until the last day until Christ returns. As examples, they cite the deaths of Stephen and David. Perhaps it depends upon the interpretation of the word "sleep" and who is doing the interpreting. Someone who has died looks like he is asleep. But they sure are not asleep when they contact you from the beyond. This is also contradicted by the New Testament which is the fulfillment and culmination of the Old. At the moment of his death, Jesus prayed, "Father, into your hands I commit my spirit!" and then "he yielded up his spirit" (Luke 23:46).

Several of the resurrection stories in the Bible describe the soul as returning to the body. This implies, of course, that the soul had left in the first place. First, there is the example of Elijah raising the widow's son from the dead. "And he stretched himself upon the child three times, and cried unto the Lord, and said, O Lord my God, I pray thee, let this child's soul come into him again. 22 And the Lord heard the voice of Elijah, and the soul of the child came into him again, and he revived" (1 Kings 17:21-22).

Science is now showing that everything in this universe vibrates and is made up of energy but at the different vibrational frequency. You, me, everything in our lives vibrates and is energy. Science is also showing that we might live in a multiverse - not a universe. If everything is energy and if our energy does not die, but simply transform to another form what happens when our human bodies die?

Do we go to another universe or to another dimension? People who have had near-death experiences have reported that all energy is connected and that we are all one. They report that everything is alive and has energy.

Near death experiences and research on past lives through regression analysis indicates that the new, transformed energy is intelligent and that we meet our loved ones who have passed away before us. In the last decade, we have seen more and more television shows, books and movies about the afterlife and about people being able to communicate with "the other side." http://www.one-mind-one-energy.com/life-after-life.html

I was in personal contact with my own father after his death. If he were in heaven or hell, I would not be able to be in contact with him. As I mentioned previously, my father and cousin d stop by on occasion. If they were in heaven or hell, they would not be able to do that, would they? My father spoke many times of being in contact with dead spirits, many of which were his deceased family members. If they were in heaven or hell they would not be traveling to this dimension. This suggests to me that they would have to be in a different dimension and able to pierce that veil to travel to this dimension.

And, of course, there are some scientists such as Dr. Robert Lanza, who believes there are such things as parallel universes and consciousness do not end at the death of the physical vehicle and that you are able to be anywhere. Lanza also believes that multiple universes can exist simultaneously. In one universe, the body can be dead. And in another it continues to exist, absorbing consciousness which migrated into this universe. This means that a dead person while traveling through the same tunnel ends up not in hell or heaven, but in a similar world he or she once inhabited, but, this time, alive. And so on, infinitely. It's almost like a cosmic Russian doll afterlife effect.

Quantum consciousness explains things like near-death experiences, astral projection, out of body experiences, and even reincarnation without needing to appeal to religious ideology. The energy of your consciousness potentially gets recycled back into a different body at some point, and in the meantime, it exists outside of the physical body on some other level of reality, and possibly in another universe.

http://www.spiritscienceandmetaphysics.com/scientists-claim-that-quantum-theory-proves-consciousness-moves-to-another-universe-at-death/#sthash.s57qlNFb.dpuf

In 2007, a physics research center was set up in Cern, Switzerland near the border to explore the origin of the universe. They had hopes of re-enacting the "Big-Bang." "A stated objective is to identify the Higgs boson, known as the 'God particle,' because of its importance to the standard model of physics, and to look for so-called supersymmetric particles, and to seek out the existence of additional dimensions."

In 2009, the Templeton Foundation awarded a prize to Bernard d'Espagnat, a French physicist at the University of Paris-Sud from the Duke of Edinburgh at Buckingham Palace for his work using theoretical physics to predict the reality of a hyper-cosmic God, who exists outside of the physical universe. So science now recognizes the existence of God as well as additional dimensions, although the Bible and other ancient Hebrew writings show recognition of their existence thousands of years ago. The Spanish scholar Nachmonides in the 12th century, studying the text of the early chapters of Genesis, concluded that they express the universe as having ten dimensions.

There are 7 Hebrew words for Heavens found in the Old Testament:

Vilon – is the word for curtain or tent as where God stretches out the heavens. (Isaiah 40:22)

Rakia – refers to the physical or visible heavens containing the sun, moon, and stars (Genesis 1:17).

Shechakim – refers to the atmosphere (Psalm 78:23).

Zevul – is the habitation where God's glory exists as in the Heavenly City (Isaiah 63:15).

Maon – is the place where angels reside from which come songs (Psalm 42:8)

Machon – refers to the storehouses where the treasures of rain, snow, and hail reside (Deuteronomy 26:15).

Aravot – is the storehouse of righteousness and peace, where angel beings reside and possibly the spirits of those not yet born in waiting (Psalm 6:4).

To our understanding, these descriptions may seem primitive, but they illustrate the revelation to the early Jews that there are unseen realities above and beyond what can be seen.

Our three-dimensional universe is not all that God created. There are other dimensions, referred to in the Bible as the heavenlies. As we have mentioned, there are seven words which are definitions of 'the heavens' in the Hebrew Bible, which, when added to the three we can perceive gives us the ten dimensions. Some of these may be populated by other beings, known as cherubim, seraphim, angels, and demons that we are unable to communicate with. We are only able to perceive and understand a small part of the whole. This is why the supernatural is so hard for us to grasp and accept. We have to be prepared to accept what we cannot see, hear or even understand and not lock ourselves into the small cave of our limited perception. Logic and reason often inhibit us from believing. We have to become like a child emerging from the womb, ready to learn and absorb the richness of the real world. http://www.understanding-the-bible.com/other-dimensions.html

Jesus said, "In my Father's house are many mansions."

Is it possible that there are other realities we are not aware of? Scientists seriously talk about things such as dimensions, multi-dimensions, parallel universes, and multi-verses, which were considered nothing more than fairy tales not so long ago.

One of the greatest mysteries of life has always been what will happen when we die. You have read many examples so far, enough so that you should not fear death if your heart belongs to God. We all owe a death, but death is not the end. We just move on to the spirit world. The big question is where is that spirit world? Is it just another dimension where we wait for judgment day, or are we immediately judged and go to either Heaven or Hell?

Science offers one explanation, and the Bible offers another. No one disputes the greatest lesson of all in life is unconditional love.

Revelations 21.1 states: 1 "And I saw a new heaven and a new earth: for the first heaven and the first earth were passed away; and there was no more sea."

Since we are not judged until after the rapture, all souls have to go someplace after their death and be held until the Lord's Second Coming. But that brings up another question. If that means that everyone that dies goes to this "Intermediate Heaven," does that also mean that the bad guys go there also until their judgment day? "Intermediate Heaven" is not to be confused with "Eternal Heaven."

Some people believe that when you die it is just the end of everything and you just take a dirt nap forever. However, Ecclesiastes 12:7 states "Then shall the dust return to the earth as it was: and the spirit shall return to God who gave it."

Most Ministers will tell you that immediately after death that your soul will go either to heaven or to hell. When Jesus was on the cross, he told the thief next to him "Today you will be with me in Paradise."

Is this a contradiction of an "Intermediate Heaven?" Is this a contradiction to when we are judged?

One of the best explanations is in the Book of Enoch. Enoch was a favorite person of God. When the angels were showing him around, Enoch in Chapter 22 said he saw four beautiful places in the West and asked what they were. The Angel Raphael responded as follows:

Enoch "22.3 Then Raphael, one of the Holy Angels who was with me, answered me and said to me: "These beautiful places are there so that the spirits, the souls of the dead, might be gathered into them. For them they were created; so that here they might gather the souls of the sons of men. 22.4 And these places they made, where they will keep them until the Day of Judgment, and until their appointed time, and that appointed time will be long until the great judgment comes upon them.

'22.5 And I saw the spirits of the sons of men who were dead and their voices reached Heaven and complained. 22.6 Then I asked Raphael, the Angel who was with me, and said to him: "Whose is this Spirit, whose voice thus reaches Heaven and complains?" 22.7 And he answered me, and said to me, saying: "This spirit is the one that came out of Abel, whom Cain, his brother, killed. And he will complain about him until his offspring are destroyed from the face of the Earth, and from amongst the offspring of men, his offspring perish." 22.8 Then I asked about him, and about judgment on all, and I said: "Why is one separated from another?" '

'22.9 And he answered me and said to me: "These three places were made, in order that they might separate the spirits of the dead. And thus, the souls of the righteous have been separated; this is the spring of water and on it the light. 22.10 Likewise, a place has been created for sinners, when they die and are buried in the earth, and judgment has not come upon them during their life. 22.11 And here their souls will be separated for this great torment, until the Great Day of Judgment and Punishment and Torment for those who curse, forever, and of vengeance on their souls. And there he will bind them forever. Verily, He is, from the beginning of the world. 22.12 And thus a place has been separated for the souls of those who complain, and give information about their destruction, about when they were killed, in the days of the sinners. 22.13 Thus a place has been created, for the souls of men who are not righteous, but sinners, accomplished in wrongdoing, and with the wrongdoers will be their lot. But their souls will not be killed on the day of judgment, nor will they rise from here."

John 14:2-3: "2 In my Father's house are many mansions: if it were not so, I would have told you. I go to prepare a place for you. 3 And if I go and prepare a place for you, I will come again, and receive you unto myself; that where I am, there ye may be also."

Jesus makes this promise to us. He is preparing a place for us in Heaven so we can live there with Him. It is up to us to accept Him in our hearts and lives.

XV

ARE THERE PHYSICAL BODIES IN HEAVEN?

We know that Christ ascended into heaven in his physical body. There are other instances mentioned in the Bible of physical bodies going to Heaven.

For instance, in Hebrews 11:5: By faith, Enoch was transmuted that he should not see death; and was not found, because God had transformed him; for before his translation he had this testimony, that he pleased God.

In the Second Book of Adam and Eve, Chapter XXII:8-9 – "8 When Enoch had ended his commandments to them, God transported him from that mountain to the land of life, to the mansions of the righteous and of the chosen, the abode of Paradise of joy, in light that reaches up to heaven; light that is outside the light of this world; for it is the light of God, that fills the whole world, but which no place can contain. 9 Thus, because Enoch was in the light of God, he found himself out of the reach of death; until God would have him die."

Enoch was the father of Methuselah and the great-grandfather of Noah. The Bible says he lived 385 years before he was taken by God. God was so pleased by Enoch that he appointed him Chief of the Archangels and Guardian of all of the celestial treasurers and the immediate attendant on God's throne. Enoch was privileged to know all of the secrets of the universe.

In 2 Kings 2:11-12: "And it came to pass, as they still went on, and talked, that behold, there appeared a chariot of fire, and horses of fire, and parted them both asunder, and Elijah went up by a whirlwind into heaven. 12. And Elisha saw it, and he cried My father, my father, the chariot of Israel, and the horsemen thereof. And he saw him no more, and he took hold of his own clothes and rent them in two pieces." Elijah's name in Hebrew means "My God is Yahweh."

In both cases, the Bible translates it as "without leaving a body behind."

Some of the research I have done says that Jesus ascended into heaven by spirit, not body. But those that say that cannot say where his body was left and neither can anyone else.

Luke 24:50-51 states: "50 And He led them out as far as to Bethany, and He lifted up His hands and blessed them. 51 And it came to pass, while He blessed them, He was parted from them, and carried up into heaven.

This ascension was carried out in front of eleven of His apostles.

An angel appeared to the apostles and told them that Jesus would appear again at His Second Coming in bodily form in the same manner as when He left.

Act 1:9-11: "9 And when He had spoken these things, while they beheld, He was taken up, and a cloud received Him out of their sight. 10 And while they looked steadfastly toward heaven as He went up, behold, two men stood by them in white apparel; 11 Which also said, Ye men of Galilee, why stand ye gazing up into heaven? This same Jesus, which is taken up from you into heaven, shall so come in like manner as ye have seen him go into heaven."

Can there be any doubt that Jesus ascended into Heaven in the physical body? In over 2000 years, man does not deny it.

XVI

HOW MANY HEAVENS ARE THERE?

The very first verse in the Bible, Genesis 1:1 states "In the beginning God created the 'heavens' and the earth." The word 'heavens' is plural. Some say the word 'heavens' means the whole universe. Does it? According to the Jewish tradition from the Torah, there were three heavens.

Psalm 102:25 states: "Of old You laid the foundation of the earth, and the heavens are the work of Your hands."

The Bible speaks of three heavens. The Bible says that the first heaven is the earth's atmosphere. The second heaven is space as far out as it stretches, and that is further than we can even possibly imagine. The third heaven is where God dwells, or what Christ referred to as his Father's House.

We now have Voyager 1 and 2 that have raced past Jupiter and Saturn and will soon leave our solar system and hopefully continue sending pictures of unknown heavens to our unseeing eyes.

Genesis 7:11-12: states that "the windows of heaven were opened. And the rain was on the earth forty days and forty nights."

Genesis 8:2: "The fountains of the deep and the windows of heaven were also stopped, and the rain from heaven was restrained"

In Deuteronomy 11:17 it says, "Then the Lord's anger will burn against you, and he will shut the heavens so that it will not rain and the ground will yield no produce...."

Again, in Deuteronomy 28:12: "The Lord will open the heavens, the storehouse of his bounty, to send rain on your land in season and to bless all the work of your hands."

There are many more scriptures that speak of the earth's atmosphere as being the first heaven.

As to the second heaven, outer space, where the stars, the sun, and the moon are, Genesis 1:17: says, "And God placed them in the Firmament of Heaven."

Several books later in Isaiah 40:22: it is said: "He stretcheth out the heavens as a curtain, and spreadeth them out as a tent to dwell in."

In Jeremiah 8:2 it goes on to say: "2 And they shall spread them before the sun, and the moon, and all the host of heaven, whom they have loved, and whom they have served, and after whom they have walked, and whom they have sought, and whom they have worshipped: they shall not be gathered, nor be buried; they shall be for dung upon the face of the earth."

According to the Bible, the third heaven is where God, the angels, and the spirits of just men live. In Deuteronomy 10:14 it states: "Behold, the heaven and the heaven of heavens is the Lord's thy God, the earth also, with all that therein is."

1 Kings 8:27 "But will God indeed dwell on the earth? behold, the heaven and heaven of heavens cannot contain thee; how much less this house that I have builded?"

In Psalms 115:16 "The heaven, even the heavens, are the Lord's: but the earth hath he given to the children of men."

The word heaven or heavens is also used in the Bible when referring to spiritual events or visions. In Acts 7:56, Stephen said, "And said,

Behold, I see the heavens opened, and the Son of man standing on the right hand of God."

After John the Baptist baptized Jesus, in Mark 1:10-11: "10 And straightway coming up out of the water, he saw the heavens opened, and the Spirit like a dove descending upon him: 11 And there came a voice from heaven, saying, Thou art my beloved Son, in whom I am well pleased."

Although the Bible refers to three heavens, the idea of seven heavens is found in Islam, Judaism, and Hinduism. In Hinduism, the god Brahma lives in the seventh heaven. However, in Islam and Judaism, the divine throne is said to be in or above the seventh heaven. It is the dwelling place of God and the angels in the Muslim and kabbalist systems.

We are all familiar with the expression "I'm in seventh heaven." Usually, it means to be in an extremely happy state, at least for a little while. Like being on "cloud nine."

The Hebrew word for heaven – shamayim – is dual in number. The perception that there are seven heavens is a very ancient myth having to do with astrology. In Babylonian mythology, the earth is a hollow half-sphere, much like a bowl — or a kufa boat — sitting upside down. Above it is the "lower firmament" or atmosphere. Then the realm of the planets, also called "sheep," "wanderers," or "watchers," as well as lightning and thunder. The wanderers also have corresponding rulers:

The Moon: Sin (AKA: Nanna, Su'en)
Mercury: Nabu (Nebo of Isaiah 46:1)
Venus: Ishtar (AKA: Astarte, Aphrodite, Artemis, Asherah of 1 Samuel 31:10)
Mars: Nergal (2 Kings 17:30)
The Sun: Shamash (AKA: Samas)
Jupiter: Marduk (patron deity of the city of Babylon, see Jeremiah 50:2)
Saturn: Ninib (possibly Nimrod of Genesis 10:8-9)

The Hindu text the Puranas also teach that there are seven higher worlds (vyahrtis or heavens) and seven lower worlds. Unlike Babylonian mythology, all the worlds are meant for humans after death. Upon death, the god of death, Yama, accounts a person's life and determines how long they will stay in which of the higher and lower worlds in accordance with the karma earned during their most recent incarnation. When the requisite stays have been accomplished, the soul is reincarnated on earth.

The Jews believe there are at least seven heavens. Originally, 2 Enoch mentioned seven "levels" of heaven; it was later changed to ten, possibly by the Eastern Orthodox Church in the 7th Century. What each of the heavens contain or represent vary depending with the teller. The story claims that Enoch walked the heavens with the angels, returned to earth and told his family, then was taken to heaven again (Genesis 5:24). The levels of heavens he visited were:

Vilon ("curtain"): a curtain which is rolled over the earth at nighttime to block the sun (Isaiah 40:22); contains the atmosphere, minor stars, snow and dew; abode of Adam and Eve; governed by Gabriel; called curtain or veil because it veils or hides the other six levels; represented by the moon.

Raqi'a/Raki'a ("expanse," "canopy"): possibly refers to the frozen canopy over the earth before the Flood (Genesis 1:7-8; Deuteronomy 11:11); Moses visited Paradise here to receive the Ten Commandments; fallen angels are imprisoned here for marrying human women (Genesis 6:4); dwelling place of souls awaiting judgment including "men of renown," apostates, tyrants; called expanse because it's where the sun and planets dwell (Genesis 1:14, 17); represented by Mercury.

Shehaquim/Shehaqim/Shehakim ("clouds"): Eden and Tree of Life, the mill that produces manna; also includes paradise and hell/hades (Psalm 78:23-24); represented by Venus.

Zebul ("habitation"): stratosphere, sun, moon, and "four great stars," including celestial mechanics; dwelling of the winds; called habitation because it's where the New Jerusalem with its temple is (Isaiah 63:15); represented by the sun.

Ma'on ("refuge"): home to "Grigori" — fallen angels who mourn for their brothers in Raqi'a; hell/Gehenna; Michael or possibly Samael presides; filled with ministering angels who sing by night; called refuge because it's where most of the angels reside; represented by Mars.

Makhon/Machon/Makon ("city," "established place"): home for angels in charge of nature's cycles and good governing systems of the world; angels who write men's actions in books; governed by Samael, a dark servant of God; storage place of rain, snow, and hail (Deuteronomy 28:12); called city because it's where the City of Angels resides; represented by Jupiter.

Araboth/Aravot ("deserts"): also known as the 10th heaven; Throne of Glory and God dwells here as well as unborn human souls, Seraphim, Cherubim, justice, righteousness, souls of the righteous, and ineffable light (Psalm 68:5); called desert because it has no moisture and no air; God also said to be above the seventh heaven; represented by Saturn.

Islam adopted the idea of seven heavens from apocryphal Jewish writings. In Islam, the word for heaven is garden. It is a place where all wishes will be fulfilled. The levels are separated by gates which can be opened if the person observed certain rituals on earth, such as jihad, charity, fasting, and pilgrimage to Mecca.

The Qur'an briefly mentions Muhammad's journey through the seven heavens, but Hadith literature describes the story more fully. Muhammad was at the Sacred Mosque in Mecca, in a half-dream state, when the angel Gabriel appeared with Buraq, the heavenly steed of the prophets. Buraq took Muhammad to the Western Wall in Jerusalem, where Muhammad prayed and was tested. When he passed the tests, Gabriel and Buraq took him on a tour of the heavens. Muhammad claimed he met several people in the different levels: 1. Adam, 2. Jesus and John the Baptist, 3. Joseph, son of Jacob, 4. the Muslim prophet Idris, 5. Aaron the priest, 6. Moses, 7. Abraham. In the seventh heaven, he also saw the Nile and the Euphrates and possibly the Tree of Life.

But it's doubtful Muhammad's story is original. In a Zoroastrianism story that pre-dates Islam by over 1000 years, the priest Arta Viraf is said to have traveled through the heavens to speak with Ormazd, the great deity of the whole universe. http://www.compellingtruth.org/seven-heavens.html

Enoch, who lived 365 years, listed Ten summaries of the Ten levels of Heavens in his II Book of Enoch.

In an ancient copy of the actual Book of Enoch:

I. The 1st Heaven – Clouds, Stars, Snow, and Morning Dew: Located atop the clouds and inhabited by winged Angels, this is where the rulers and elders of the constellations reside here with 200 angels. Nearby is the Great Sea, larger than any of earth's oceans, while the Heavenly store-houses for both snow and morning dew are located here. (II Enoch 3:1, 4:1, 5:1, 6:1)

II. The 2nd Heaven – Prison of Darkness, Death, and Despair: A place of darkness where the angels of darkness who joined with Satan in his original rebellion have been imprisoned, hanging from chains and awaiting Judgment Day. (II Enoch 7:1-3)

III. The 3rd Heaven – Mercy of Paradise and Justice of Hell: A Paradise reserved for the good and the righteous, consisting of a fragrant orchard grove with the fiery golden Tree of Life in the center where the Lord rests when visiting. The roots to the Tree of Life extend downwards to the Garden of Eden below and there four different springs flowing with milk, honey, wine, and oil. 300 singing Angels tend the Garden. In contrast, the northern section is a terrible place of icy, frozen darkness with a river of fire flowing through it and inhabited by fierce, cruel angels with weapons who torture those sinners who have been condemned here. (II Enoch 8:1-10, 9:1, 10:1-3)

IV. The 4th Heaven – Twelve Gates of the Sun and the Moon: Includes the 12 great gates (and pathways) of the Moon, the six eastern gates and six western gates of the Sun along with all its different pathways. Guarded and maintained by thousands upon thousands of Angels, the sun is escorted daily by 8,000 other stars and needs 100 Angels just to light its fire Some of the inhabitants include six-winged creatures who accompany the Angels, exotic Rainbow-colored Phoenixes and Chalkydri with heads like crocodiles, as well as armed soldiers who are constantly singing and playing musical instruments. (II Enoch 11:1-6, 12:1-2, 13:1-2, 14:1-2, 15:1-3, 16:1-3, 17:1)

V. The 5th Heaven – Giants of Silence, Sadness, and Regret: A sad, solemn place of silence and gloom filled with a countless number of gigantic human soldiers called the Grigori who chose Satan as their prince and rejected the Lord of light. Their faces are withered, but they still remain capable of occasionally singing praises unto the LORD. (II Enoch 18:1-7)

VI. The 6th Heaven – Archangels of the Arts and Sciences: Traditional home of seven different groups of Angels who both rule over the stars, keeping track of their motions, as well overseeing and managing the various governments on Earth. They also keep records of everyone's good or bad deeds and keep careful watch over earth's natural systems of life and death. Other inhabitants include six Phoenixes, six Cherubim, six Seraphim, who, with one voice, sing songs so other-worldly, they remain impossible to describe. (II Enoch 19:1-3)

VII. The 7th Heaven – Powers and Dominions of Fire and Light: An Angelic realm of light and fire, filled with the many different eternally loyal soldiers of the Lord including Archangels, Virtues (forces), Dominions, Powers, (orders), and Principalities (governments). Also present are the other-worldly Cherubim, seraphim, thrones, and other celestial being with many eyes, along with what the text calls 'nine regiments' and the 'stations of light.' (II Enoch 20:1-2, 21:3)

VIII. The 8th Heaven – Summer and Winter of Drought and Snow: Controls and changes the different seasons of the year causing either draught or rain on Earth. Also contains the twelve constellations. (II Enoch 21:7)

IX. The 9th Heaven – Twelve Secret Mansions of the Stars in the Night: Considered the celestial homes of the constellations which lie both above and behind the 12 groups of stars as seen in the circular night sky above the Earth. Called Kuchavim in Hebrew. (II Enoch 21:8)

X. The 10th Heaven – Cherubim, Seraphim, and the Throne of Thunder and Lightning: Seen as the highest of Heavens as well as the actual location of the Lord God's mighty Throne of Judgment. Typically, this is where the Lord holds counsel with His Angels and Saints, making His decisions, handing down His judgments, and commanding His countless Angels who surround Him as they sing songs of praise and glory. (II Enoch 22:1-10)
https://stjudasmaccabaeus.wordpress.com/2011/02/25/apocfypha-the-10-heavens-of-the-2nd-book-of-enoch-i-i-enoch/

Enoch described Heaven in the Book of Enoch, Chapter 78. In 78.2 he was describing the moon as having four names: Asonya, Ebla, Benase, and Era'e. In 78.3 he stated "These are two great lights (sun and moon); their disc is like the disc of Heaven and in size the two are equal. This indicates to me that Heaven is a planet of sorts, not just space or a dimension. The Bible also refers often to the sun and the moon which would indicate Heaven is in our solar system.

The Third Heaven sounds like the place where we all go as an intermediate heaven to wait until Judgment Day. Jesus told the thief on the cross that this day you will be with me in Paradise. Jesus goes to the Third Heaven to visit. The Third Heaven is called Mercy of Paradise and Justice of Hell.

XVII

REWARDS IN HEAVEN

In Revelations 22:12, Jesus said, "And, behold, I come quickly; and my reward is with me, to give every man according as his work shall be." According to the Bible, rewards will be distributed differently to each person according to the work that we have done for Christ. Good works will not get you into heaven, but by being saved and going to heaven, you will be rewarded for your good works. We can only be saved by grace through our faith in Jesus Christ.

First and most importantly, every single person on this earth will have to appear before the Judgment Seat of Jesus Christ – no exceptions – and be judged for everything that you have ever done or said down here on this earth. The Bible Verse for this is 2 Corinthians 5:10: "10 For we must all appear before the judgment seat of Christ; that every one may receive the things done in his body, according to that he hath done, whether it be good or bad."

Without God's grace, I will never make it. I try to live a good life, but my mouth is always getting me in trouble. I am forever saying I am sorry and asking God's forgiveness.

In 1 Corinthians 3:8 Paul said: "Now he that planteth and he that watereth are one: and every man shall receive his own reward according to his own labour."

If you go to Revelations 2:23, it reads "And I will kill her children with death; and all the churches shall know that I am he which searcheth the reins and hearts: and I will give unto every one of you according to your works."

And it sounds like God has something special in mind for missionaries and evangelists. In Mark 10:29-30 it states: "And Jesus answered and said, Verily I say unto you, there is no man that hath left house, or brethren, or sisters, or father, or mother, or wife, or children, or lands, for my sake, and the gospel's, 30 But he shall receive an hundredfold now in this time, houses, and brethren, and sisters, and mothers, and children, and lands, with persecutions; and in the world to come eternal life."

CROWNS AS REWARDS

According to the Bible, there are five crowns and rewards in heaven. The first Crown is the Crown of Righteousness for those believers who were ready and waiting for the return of Jesus Christ. In 2 Timothy 4:8 it speaks of the Crown of Righteousness as "7 I have fought a good fight, I have finished my course, I have kept the faith: 8 Henceforth there is laid up for me a crown of righteousness, which the Lord, the righteous judge, shall give me at that day: and not to me only, but unto all them also that love his appearing." It is given to those that love the Lord and wait for his return. It is not for those that depend upon their own works. It is for those that have a passionate desire to be with the Lord.

The next crown is the incorruptible crown – The Victor's Crown. This crown is for those that discipline their bodies and have had self-control. It is referred to in 1 Corinthians 9:25 which states: "And every man that striveth for the mastery is temperate in all things. Now they do it to obtain a corruptible crown, but we are incorruptible. 26 I therefore so run, not as uncertainly; so fight I, not as one that beateth the air: 27 But I keep under my body, and bring it into subjection: lest that by any means, when I have preached to others, I myself should be a castaway. " 2 Timothy 4: 7 I have fought a good fight, I have finished my course, I have kept the faith:" This has also been referred to as the Runner's Crown and the Worker's Crown.

The third crown is the Crown of Life – the Martyr's Crown. It is for those who patiently endured testings, temptations, and trials. This Crown is promised us in James 1:12 when James told us, "12 Blessed is the man that endureth temptation: for when he is tried, he shall receive the crown of life, which the Lord hath promised to them that love him. It was mentioned again in Revelation 2:10 "10 Fear none of those things which thou shalt suffer: behold, the devil shall cast some of you into prison, that ye may be tried; and ye shall have tribulation ten days: be thou faithful unto death, and I will give thee a crown of life." Being faithful in spite of your trials and tribulations will give you the Crown of Life. It is for those that keep all of God's Commandments.

The fourth crown is the Crown of Glory – The Elder's Crown. This is a crown for Leaders, Pastors, Elders, Teachers who were Godly Examples to the Flock of Believers that were entrusted and assigned to their care. This is referred to in 1 Peter 5: 2 where it says: "2 Feed the flock of God which is among you, taking the oversight thereof, not by constraint, but willingly; not for filthy lucre, but of a ready mind; 3 Neither as being Lords over God's heritage, but being ensamples to the flock. 4 And when the chief Shepherd shall appear, ye shall receive a crown of glory that fadeth not away." This word also means that the praise and honor we bestow to God alone is due Him because of who He is (Isaiah 42:8, 48:11; Galatians 1:5). It also recognizes that believers are incredibly blessed to enter into the kingdom, into the very likeness of Christ Himself. For as Paul so eloquently put it, "For I consider that the sufferings of this present time are not worthy to be compared with the glory which shall be revealed in us" (Romans 8:18 NKJV). http://www.gotquestions.org/heavenly-crowns.html

The fifth crown is the Crown of Rejoicing. This is the soul winner's crown. The Crown of Rejoicing is referred to in 1 Thessalonians 2:19 where it says: "19 For what is our hope, or joy, or crown of rejoicing? Are not even ye in the presence of our Lord Jesus Christ at his coming?" This is where God will wipe away every tear, where there will be no more pain, death or sorrow for anyone.

Some say we will receive a Crown of Separation of Crown of Holiness and a Crown of Protection for the righteous person.

We are warned to be careful and not to go out in the world and lose our rewards. In 1 John 1:7-8, the Bible states: "7 For many deceivers are entered into the world, who confess not that Jesus Christ is come in the flesh. This is a deceiver and an antichrist. 8 Look to yourselves, that we lose not those things which we have wrought, but that we receive a full reward." You can lose your crown just by doing a good deed with a wrong motive.

Revelation 4:4 describes heaven and the Crowns of Glory as "4 And round about the throne were four and twenty seats: and upon the seats I saw four and twenty elders sitting, clothed in white raiment; and they had on their heads crowns of gold." And in verses 10 and 11 they bowed down before Jesus and took off their crowns and cast them before Him and said "11 Thou art worthy, O Lord, to receive glory and honour and power: for thou hast created all things, and for thy pleasure they are and were created."

In 1 Corinthians 40-44 it states as follows: "40 There are also celestial bodies, and bodies terrestrial: but the glory of the celestial is one, and the glory of the terrestrial is another. 41 There is one glory of the sun, and another glory of the moon, and another glory of the stars: for one star differeth from another star in glory. 42 So also is the resurrection of the dead. It is sown in corruption; it is raised in incorruption: 43 It is sown in dishonour; it is raised in glory: it is sown in weakness; it is raised in power: 44 It is sown a natural body; it is raised a spiritual body. There is a natural body, and there is a spiritual body.

Since we do not have actual bodies in heaven, but spirits, we cannot have actual crowns, can we? So that would seem to suggest that

I Corinthians means that the different crowns might signify that our souls will shine differently according to the type crown we are rewarded; or not.

Some say in heaven we'll have new bodies which are both spiritual, or can be material – can materialize or dematerialize, can travel with the speed of thought and have powers that even the angels have yet to learn – No traffic problems, we'll just fly through each other – Through walls, doors, people, anything!

Another reward is the mansion that Jesus is preparing for us. In John 14:2 Jesus said: "2 In my Father's house are many mansions: if it were not so, I would have told you. I go to prepare a place for you." If we were just spirits without bodies, why would we need mansions or shelter or any kind?

Years ago in this little church we sang an old song called "Lord Build me a Cabin in the Corner of Glory Land." I think it has been 55 or so years since I have heard that old song, but I remember the last time it was sung one of the church members stood up and said she was offended by it because Jesus promised her a mansion and she did not want a cabin someplace in the corner of Glory Land, she wanted a big mansion. I always thought it was a song of humility. I would be happy with a cabin if the Lord granted me entrance into Heaven. I am a perpetual sinner and to think he loved me enough to let me in the door to stay makes my eternal day.

XVIII

GOING TO HEAVEN

Absolutely everyone, when they die, will have to stand before God. No one can avoid it. We are not judged by our good deeds. We are judged by our faith in Jesus Christ. We must account for all of our thoughts and deeds and actions.

In Romans 14:10-12 Jesus stated: "10 But why dost thou judge thy brother? or why dost thou set at nought thy brother? for we shall all stand before the judgment seat of Christ. 11 For it is written, As I live, saith the Lord, every knee shall bow to me, and every tongue shall confess to God. 12 So then every one of us shall give account of himself to God."

Ephesians 2:8-9 states: "For by grace are you saved through faith and that not of yourselves; it is the gift of God; 9. Not of works, lest any man shouldst boast."

There is a Judgment of Faith and a Judgment of Works that will determine what our rewards will be. The work we do for our Lord in this lifetime does not affect our salvation or our Judgment or Faith, but it does affect the rewards we reap in the afterlife.

God keeps a record in Heaven of all of our deeds, good and bad. As I grow older, my memory is not so good. Unfortunately, one day I will again be reminded of all of those things I have long forgotten and have to answer for them all.

Do people in heaven see what is happening on Earth?

Yes. This is revealed in reading Revelation 19:1-2 where it says: "And after these things I heard a great voice of much people in heaven, saying, Alleluia; Salvation, and glory, and honour, and power, unto the Lord our God: 2 For true and righteous are his judgments: for he hath judged the great whore, which did corrupt the earth with her fornication, and hath avenged the blood of his servants at her hand."

Also in Luke 28 "And it came to pass about an eight days after these sayings, he took Peter and John and James and went up into a mountain to pray. 29 And as he prayed, the fashion of his countenance was altered, and his raiment was white and glistering. 30 And, behold, there talked with him two men, which were Moses and Elias: 31 Who appeared in glory, and spake of his decease which he should accomplish at Jerusalem. 32 But Peter and they that were with him were heavy with sleep: and when they were awake, they saw his glory and the two men that stood with him. 33 And it came to pass, as they departed from him, Peter said unto Jesus, Master, it is good for us to be here: and let us make three tabernacles; one for thee, and one for Moses, and one for Elias: not knowing what he said. 34 While he thus spake, there came a cloud, and overshadowed them: and they feared as they entered into the cloud. 35 And there came a voice out of the cloud, saying, This is my beloved Son: hear him."

And again, in Luke 15:10 where it states "Likewise, I say unto you, there is joy in the presence of the angels of God over one sinner that repenteth."

What is heaven like? The Bible describes it as gardens, cities, a Kingdom. God's Kingdom will come to the new Earth. We will see things we cannot imagine. Isaiah 6 King James Version. "In the year that King Uzziah died I saw also the Lord sitting upon a throne, high and lifted up, and his train filled the temple. 2 Above it stood the seraphims:

each one had six wings; with twain he covered his face, and with twain he covered his feet, and with twain he did fly."

Revelations 21:10-10 "And he carried me away in the spirit to a great and high mountain, and shewed me that great city, the holy Jerusalem, descending out of heaven from God, 11 Having the glory of God: and her light was like unto a stone most precious, even like a jasper stone, clear as crystal; 12 And had a wall great and high, and had twelve gates, and at the gates twelve angels, and names written thereon, which are the names of the twelve tribes of the children of Israel: 13 On the east three gates; on the north three gates; on the south three gates; and on the west three gates. 14 And the wall of the city had twelve foundations, and in them the names of the twelve apostles of the Lamb. 15 And he that talked with me had a golden reed to measure the city, and the gates thereof, and the wall thereof. 16 And the city lieth foursquare, and the length is as large as the breadth: and he measured the city with the reed, twelve thousand furlongs. The length and the breadth and the height of it are equal. 17 And he measured the wall thereof, an hundred and forty and four cubits, according to the measure of a man, that is, of the angel. 18 And the building of the wall of it was of jasper: and the city was pure gold, like unto clear glass. 19 And the foundations of the wall of the city were garnished with all manner of precious stones. The first foundation was jasper; the second, sapphire; the third, a chalcedony; the fourth, an emerald; 20 The fifth, sardonyx; the sixth, sardius; the seventh, chrysolyte; the eighth, beryl; the ninth, a topaz; the tenth, a chrysoprasus; the eleventh, a jacinth; the twelfth, an amethyst. 21 And the twelve gates were twelve pearls: every several gate was of one pearl: and the street of the city was pure gold, as it were transparent glass. 22 And I saw no temple therein: for the Lord God Almighty and the Lamb are the temple of it. 23 And the city had no need of the sun, neither of the moon, to shine in it: for the glory of God did lighten it, and the Lamb is the light thereof. 24 And the nations of them which are saved shall walk in the light of it: and the kings of the earth do bring their glory and honour into it. 25 And the gates of it shall not be shut at all by day: for there shall be no night there. 26 And they shall bring the glory and honour of the nations into it. 27 And there shall in no wise enter into it anything that defileth, neither whatsoever worketh abomination, or maketh a lie: but they which are written in the Lamb's book of life."

The Bible speaks of crowns and thrones in Heaven, so that indicates that there will be different functions and different levels of responsibility assigned to different people in Heaven. There will still be different levels of order and structure throughout God's Universe.

"There is also going to be an extension of man's mind beyond what we know and understand now. There will be an opening of understanding into the secrets and mysteries of the universe. Furthermore, in heaven there will be no fear of any kind of evil, and God will provide magnificently for His people." http://www1.cbn.com/questions/describe-heaven

In 1 Corinthians 6:3 it states that we will even judge fallen angels or demons. "3 Know ye not that we shall judge angels? how much more things that pertain to this life?"

Christ refers to Hell as an actual place. The Bible says that the wicked suffer continuously and are consciously aware of their suffering. The Bible says you retain all of your reasoning, your desires, and all of your memories. You constantly yearn for relief but cannot be comforted and have no hope.

Psalms 9:17 – "The wicked shall be turned into hell and all the nations that forget God." We need to pray for this country. We need to pray that when people vote that they will vote their religion and religious morals instead of what the government will give them free.

Revelations 20:14 – "And death and hell were cast into the lake of fire. This is the second death."

There are 54 verses in the Bible describing Hell. Hell is a place of fire. It is real, not just some place talked about by Christians. People that have had near-death experiences have described it.

In Matthew 13:42 Jesus said, "And shall cast them into a furnace of fire: there shall be wailing and gnashing of teeth."

Revelations 20-15 states: "And whosoever was not found written in the book of life was cast into the lake of fire."

The Bible tells us that Hell is inside the earth. Matthew 12:40 states: "For as Jonas was three days and three nights in the whale's belly; so shall the Son of man be three days and three nights in the heart of the earth."

Ephesians 4:9 states: "Now that he ascended, what is it but that he also descended first into the lower parts of the earth?"

On April 10, 1987, a Birmingham, Alabama newspaper printed an article entitled "Earth's Center Hotter Than Sun's Surface, Scientists Say". This article stated that the earth's inner core has a temperature of over 12,000 degrees Fahrenheit.

Jesus referred to Hell in different ways. He called it everlasting fire, eternal damnation, resurrection of damnation, the furnace of fire, the fire that shall never be quenched, tormented in the flame, place of torment, outer darkness, and everlasting punishment among others.

It is a lake of fire that you cannot crawl from. If you are there, it is because you chose to be there in your lifetime. You have another option. In the sixteenth chapter of Luke, the rich man died and went to hell. He saw Abraham off in the distance and yelled for him to send Lazarus with some water to cool his tongue. Abraham refused and reminded the rich man that Lazarus had a hard life and the rich man had an easy life. The rich man then asked Abraham to send Lazarus to his house to testify to his five brothers so they would not end up in Hell.

And Jesus told his disciples in Matthew 19:22-26 "22 But when the young man heard that saying, he went away sorrowful: for he had great possessions. 23 Then said Jesus unto his disciples, Verily I say unto you, that a rich man shall hardly enter into the kingdom of heaven. 24 And again I say unto you, it is easier for a camel to go through the eye of a needle than for a rich man to enter into the kingdom of God. 25 When his disciples heard [it], they were exceedingly amazed, saying, who then can be saved? 26 But Jesus beheld [them], and said unto them, with men this is impossible; but with God all things are possible."

But you can know you are going to Heaven.

First, you must believe in God and that Jesus Christ is the son of God. You must believe that Jesus died for your sins and arose from the grave.

Next, you must ask Jesus to forgive you of your sins and then accept Jesus as your Lord and Savior.

A simple prayer might be as follows: Dear Jesus. I believe that You died for me. I believe that You paid for my sins on the cross. I believe that You rose from the dead. I ask You to forgive me of my sins. I ask You to wash me clean of all sin. I put my faith and trust in You as my only hope for living eternally with You in heaven. I ask You to be my Savior and my Lord. I want to live my life for Jesus Christ. I understand that my salvation is not based on my works but the sacrifice of Jesus on the cross and Your grace. I ask you to come into my heart and to live in my life. Thank You for saving me! Amen!

This is a total commitment of your life to Jesus and to live your life for Him from now on. This means you won't swear anymore or watch movies that have swearing in them. If necessary, you will either ask your friends to not swear in front of you or else you will find that you will be changing your friends.

You will start reading the Bible daily even if it is just a few verses or just one chapter per day. You will say prayers morning and night. You will find that you will be praying throughout the day because your life has become dependent upon God. You will find that He runs your life better than you ever did.

You will probably start looking for a church to attend so you can meet others that believe the way that you now do and you can get your soul nourished each week. This may take up to a year to find the church you are comfortable attending. Or at least you will watch church on television on Sunday morning.

Your routine has changed, your friends have changed, you have the world by the tail, and you wake up and find out that you are very happy and feel grateful all the time.

XIX

WHAT IS HELL

There are 162 references to *hell* in the New Testament. In the Old Testament *hell* is referred to as Shoel. In the New Testament, hell is referred to as Hades.

At Luke 16:22 Jesus told of the rich man that went to hell: "22 And it came to pass, that the beggar died, and was carried by the angels into Abraham's bosom: the rich man also died and was buried; 23 And in hell he lifted up his eyes, being in torments, and seeth Abraham afar off, and Lazarus in his bosom. 24 And he cried and said, Father Abraham, have mercy on me, and send Lazarus, that he may dip the tip of his finger in water, and cool my tongue; for I am tormented in this flame. 25 But Abraham said, Son, remember that thou in thy lifetime receivedst thy good things, and likewise Lazarus evil things: but now he is comforted, and thou art tormented."

You will note that the rich man said he was being tormented in this "flame."

In Matthew 13:42, Jesus said "42 And shall cast them into a furnace of fire: there shall be wailing and gnashing of teeth." Here it was called a "furnace of fire."

At Matthew 25:41 Jesus said: "41 Then shall he say also unto them on the left hand, depart from me, ye cursed, into everlasting fire, prepared for the devil and his angels." Here hell was referred to as "everlasting fire."

And then in Revelation 20:25 it says: "15 And whosoever was not found written in the book of life was cast into the lake of fire." You will note in this verse hell is referred to as the "lake of fire."

Not only does the Bible indicate that Hell will be on Earth, but the Book of Enoch also indicates that Hell is on Earth.

Enoch XVIII:1 states: "1. And they took [and] brought me to a place in which those who were there were like flaming fire, and, when they wished, they appeared as men. 2. And they brought me to the place of darkness, and to a mountain the point of whose summit reached to heaven. 3. And I saw the places of the luminaries [and the treasuries of the stars] and of the thunder [and] in the uttermost depths, where were a fiery bow and arrows and their quiver, and [[a fiery sword]] and all the lightnings. 4. And they took me to the living waters, and to the fire of the west, which receives every setting of the sun. 5. And I came to a river of fire in which the fire flows like water and discharges itself into the great sea towards the west. 6. I saw the great rivers and came to the great [river and to the great] darkness and went to the place where no flesh walks. 7. I saw the mountains of the darkness of winter and the place whence all the waters of the deep flow. 8. I saw the mouths of all the rivers of the earth and the mouth of the deep." I saw the treasuries of all the winds: I saw how He had furnished with them the whole creation and the firm foundations of the earth. 2. And I saw the corner-stone of the earth: I saw the four winds which bear [the earth and] the firmament of the heaven. 3. [[And I saw how the winds stretch out the vaults of heaven]], and have their station between heaven and earth: [[these are the pillars of the heaven]]. 4. I saw the winds of heaven which turn and bring the circumference of the sun and all the stars to their setting. 5. I saw the winds on the earth carrying the clouds: I saw [[the paths of the angels. I saw]] at the end of the earth the firmament of the heaven above. And I proceeded and saw a place which burns day and night, where there are seven mountains of magnificent stones, three towards the east, and three towards the south. 7. And as for those towards the east, <one> was of coloured stone, and one of pearl, and one of jacinth, and those towards the south of red stone. 8. But the middle one reached to heaven like the throne of God, of alabaster, and the summit of the throne was of sapphire. 9. And I saw a flaming fire. And beyond these mountains 10. is a region the end of the great earth: there the heavens were completed. 11. And I saw a deep abyss, with columns [[of heavenly fire, and among them I saw columns]] of fire fall, which were beyond measure alike towards the height and towards the depth. 12. And beyond that abyss I saw a place which had no firmament of the heaven above, and no firmly founded earth beneath it: there was no water upon it, and no birds, but it was a waste and horrible place. 13. I saw there seven stars like great burning mountains, and to me, when I inquired regarding them, 14. The angel said: 'This place is the end of heaven and earth: this has become a prison for the stars and the host of heaven. 15. And the stars which roll over the fire are they which have transgressed the commandment of the Lord in the beginning of their rising, because they did not come forth at their appointed times. 16. And He was wroth with them and bound them till the time when their guilt should be consummated (even) [for ten thousand years].'"

Enoch Chapter XXI. "1. And I proceeded to where things were chaotic. 2. And I saw there something horrible: I saw neither a heaven above nor a firmly founded earth, but a place chaotic and horrible. 3. And there I saw seven stars of the heaven bound together in it, like great mountains and burning with fire. 4. Then I said: 'For what sin are they bound, and on what account have they been cast in hither?' 5. Then said Uriel, one of the holy angels, who was with me, and was chief over them, and said: 'Enoch, why dost thou ask, and why art thou eager for the truth? 6. These are of the number of the stars [of heaven], which have transgressed the commandment of the Lord, and are bound here till ten thousand years, the time entailed by their sins, are consummated.' 7. And from thence I went to another place, which was still more horrible than the former, and I saw a horrible thing: a great fire there which burnt and blazed, and the place was cleft as far as the abyss, being full of great descending columns of fire: neither its extent or magnitude could I see, nor could I conjecture. 8. Then I said: 'How fearful is the place and how terrible to look upon!' 9. Then Uriel answered me, one of the holy angels who was with me, and said unto me: 'Enoch, why hast thou such fear and affright?' And I answered: 'Because of this fearful place, and because of the spectacle of the pain.' 10. And he said [[unto me]]: 'This place is the prison of the angels, and here they will be imprisoned forever.'"

Enoch CHAPTER XXIII. "1. From thence I went to another place to the west of the ends of the earth. 2. And I saw a [[burning]] fire which ran without resting and paused not from its course day or night but (ran) regularly. 3. And I asked saying: 'What is this which rests not?' 4. Then Raguel, one of the holy angels who was with me, answered me [[and said unto me]]: 'This course [of fire] [[which thou hast seen]] is the fire in the west which †persecutes† all the luminaries of heaven.'"

And getting to what is important to you, in Chapters XXIV and XXV, and Chapter XXVII, Enoch tells us: "1. And I went from thence to the middle of the earth, and I saw a blessed place [in which there were trees] with branches abiding and blooming [of a dismembered tree]. 2. And there I saw a holy mountain, [[and]] underneath the mountain to the east there was a stream and it flowed towards the south. 3. And I saw towards the east another mountain higher than this, and between them a deep and narrow ravine: in it also ran a stream [underneath] the mountain. 4. And to the west thereof there was another mountain, lower than the former and of small elevation, and a ravine [deep and dry] between them: and another deep and dry ravine was at the extremities of the three [mountains]. 5. And all the ravines were deep [[and narrow]], (being formed) of hard rock, and trees were not planted upon them. 6. And I marveled [[at the rocks, and I marveled]] at the ravine, yea, I marveled very much."

Enoch Chapter XXVII:1 "1. Then said I: 'For what object is this blessed land, which is entirely filled with trees, and this accursed valley [[between]]?' 2. [[Then Uriel, one of the holy angels who was with me, answered and said: 'This]] accursed valley is for those who are accursed forever: Here shall all [the accursed] be gathered together who utter with their lips against the Lord unseemly words and of His glory speak hard things. 3. In the last days there shall be upon them the spectacle of righteous judgment in the presence of the righteous forever: here shall the merciful bless the Lord of glory, the Eternal King. 4. In the days of judgment over the former, they shall bless Him for the mercy in accordance with which He has assigned them (their lot).' 5. Then I blessed the Lord of Glory and set forth His [glory] and lauded Him gloriously."

"So far as we can tell from Scripture, the present hell, is somewhere in the heart of the earth itself. It is also called 'the pit' (Isa. 14:9, 15: Ezek. 32:18-21) and 'the abyss' (Rev. 9:2)...

'The writers certainly themselves believed hell to be real and geographically 'beneath' the earth's surface. . . To say this is not scientific is to assume science knows much more about the earth's interior than is actually the case. The great 'pit' [hell] would only need to be about 100 miles or less in diameter to contain, with much room to spare, all the forty billion or so people who have ever lived, assuming their 'spiritual' bodies are the same size as their physical bodies." (Henry M. Morris, The Bible Has the Answer, p. 220)

'The Birmingham News, April 10, 1987 had an article entitled "Earth's Center Hotter Than Sun's Surface, Scientists Say". The article stated that scientists have recently discovered, "The Earth's Inner Core has a Temperature of over 12,000 Degrees Fahrenheit!" Have you seen pictures of a volcano erupting, spewing a lake of fire from inside the earth — consuming everything within miles just from the heat? When Mount St. Helens erupted in May 18, 1980, it was described by reporters, "when HELL surfaced upon the earth." The book, Volcanoes, Earth's Awakening (p.91) describes an erupting volcano as "descent into HELL".

'Thousands of years ago, the Bible described a place called hell in the heart of the earth that matches exactly what science is discovering....

'In Numbers 16, the Bible gives the account of people falling into hell alive!

"And the Earth opened her mouth and swallowed them up, and their houses, and all the men that appertained unto Korah, and all their goods. They, and all that appertained to them, went down alive into the pit, and the Earth closed upon them." Numbers 16:32-33

'Caspar Peucer, a famous fourteenth century astronomer and physician, who also researched and documented the volcanoe eruptions at Heklafell wrote some very frightening information in his research findings. Peucer, claims (as others) that "fearful howlings, weeping and gnashing of teeth" could be heard "for many miles. . ." as these volcanoes erupted:

"Out of the bottomless abyss of Heklafell, or rather out of Hell itself, rise melancholy cries and loud wailings, so that these can be heard for many miles around. . . there may be heard in the mountain fearful howlings, weeping and gnashing of teeth."

'(Haraldur Sigurdsson, Melting the Earth, The History of Ideas on Volcanic Eruptions, p. 73)

'And Caspar Peucer is not alone. There are others who believe they have heard "cries and screaming" coming from volcanoes. Most have tried to ignore the obvious. Some simply explain the "sounds of hell" to some rational meaning. But they are there. . .

"The fearsome noises that issued from some of their volcanoes were certainly thought to be the screams of tormented souls in the fires of hell below".

'(Haraldur Sigurdsson, Melting the Earth, The History of Ideas on Volcanic Eruptions, p. 73)

'Inside this earth, this very moment, there are millions of lost, tormented souls — burning, weeping, wailing — without any hope whatsoever!

'In Mark 9:46, Jesus Christ says about hell: "Where their worm dieth not, and the fire is not quenched."

'Jesus said explicitly — Their worm — not a worm, or the worm — but their worm. The Bible teaches that Christians will one day have a body like the Lord Jesus Christ. Could it be, as some Bible students teach — that men and women in hell take on the form of their father, Satan (John 8:44)? In Revelation 12:3, Satan is described as a red dragon.

Could Jesus Christ be referring to the body lost men and women will have for eternity?

'The earth's crust on land is normally 50 miles thick. You'd have to go down 50 miles before the edge of the fire. But in parts of the ocean floor, the earth's crust is less than a mile thick.

'Scientists recently discovered cracks on the ocean floor where fire was leaking out. Do you know what they found around these fire-breathing vents in the crust? Eight-foot long worms, found no other place in the world! The book, The Deep Sea, by Joseph Wallace (p.39), reads, "Perhaps the strangest of ocean creatures recently discovered are Riftia, the giant tube worms. Measuring up to 8 feet in length, the worms are only found near deep sea vents."

'And Jesus Christ said, "Where their worm dieth not, and the fire is not quenched."

'Have you read Isaiah 66 where the Lord Jesus Christ is quoting Mark 9:46? Look at the context and time period of Isaiah 66:22-24: Isaiah 66:22-24: 22 For as the new heavens and the new earth, which I will make, shall remain before me, saith the LORD, so shall your seed and your name remain. 23 And it shall come to pass, that from one new moon to another, and from one sabbath to another, shall all flesh come to worship before me, saith the Lord. 24 And they shall go forth, and look upon the carcasses of the men that have transgressed against me: for their worm shall not die, neither shall their fire be quenched; and they shall be an abhorring unto all flesh. The "new heavens and new earth" of Isaiah 66:22 matches Revelation 21:1. This occurs after the Great White Throne Judgement of Revelation 20:10-15! The references to "carcasses"; "their worm"; "their fire" (vs 24) — is after the Great White Throne Judgement of the lost people! The reference to ". the men that have transgressed. . ." are the lost people after the Great White Throne Judgement. And at this point — they have received their new body! Notice what Isaiah says, the saved people shall "look upon the carcasses of the men that have transgressed. . ." It's worth mentioning that a "carcass" is not always a "dead body". For instance, two times the Bible specifically uses the term "dead carcass" (Deut. 14:8 and Ezekiel 6:5). If a carcass is always a "dead" body, then why say "dead" carcass.

And there's nothing in the context of Isaiah to imply these "men that transgressed" are "dead."

'In fact, Isaiah clearly says, "their worm shall not die." Even in our language, we refer to a living body as a "carcass". For example, "Get your carcass [body] in here". Why is that important? Because when the saved people in Isaiah 66:24 are "looking upon the carcasses of the men that have transgressed" — And do you know what they are seeing? "Their worm"! The "carcass" they are seeing is "their Worm that shall not die". The end of Isaiah 66:24 is a frightening endorsement of this interpretation. What the saved people are viewing Isaiah says is, ". . . an abhorring unto all flesh". And my friend, that is not JUST a normal flesh body they are looking at! It is something that will send chills screaming through your soul at the horror. And it will happen!

'And it will happen to you if you die without the Lord Jesus Christ!

'Even though the world tries to extinguish the cries and reality of hell — the truth of hell echoes throughout our world. We desperately pretend to cover our ears and ignore the "screams, the weeping, the wailing, the gnashing of teeth" but it is there. . . And we know it. We refuse to accept such a place exist. But it is there. And we know it. Nothing we can do, nothing we can say, can erase the horror of hell from our minds.

'It is there. And we know it." http://www.av1611.org/hell.html

Regardless of where you believe the physical location of Hell is, it is much more important for you to constantly keep in mind that there is a need to avoid going there.

XX

DO ANIMALS GO TO HEAVEN?

When the Bible describes Heaven in the book of Revelation, it describes Horses coming into and out of Heaven.

Revelation 6:2-8 – "And I saw, and behold a white horse: and he that sat on him had a bow; and a crown was given unto him: and he went forth conquering, and to conquer. 2 And I saw, and behold a white horse: and he that sat on him had a bow, and a crown was given unto him: and he went forth conquering, and to conquer. 3 And when he had opened the second seal, I heard the second beast say, Come and see. 4 And there went out another horse that was red: and power was given to him that sat thereon to take peace from the earth, and that they should kill one another: and there was given unto him a great sword. 5 And when he had opened the third seal, I heard the third beast say, Come and see. And I beheld, and lo a black horse, and he that sat on him had a pair of balances in his hand. 6 And I heard a voice in the midst of the four beasts say, a measure of wheat for a penny, and three measures of barley for a penny; and see thou hurt not the oil and the wine. 7 And when he had opened the fourth seal, I heard the voice of the fourth beast say, Come and see. 8 And I looked and behold a pale horse: and his name that sat on him was Death, and Hell followed with him. And power was given unto them over the fourth part of the earth, to kill with sword, and with hunger, and with death, and with the beasts of the earth."

Revelations 19:11 – "And I saw heaven opened, and behold a white horse, and he that sat upon him was called Faithful and True, and in righteousness, he doth judge and make war."

Revelation 19:14 – "And the armies [which were] in heaven followed him upon white horses, clothed in fine linen, white and clean."

In Zechariah 6:   1 "And I turned, and lifted up mine eyes, and looked, and, behold, there came four chariots out from between two mountains, and the mountains were mountains of brass. 2 In the first chariot were red horses; and in the second chariot black horses; 3 And in the third chariot white horses; and in the fourth chariot grisled and bay horses. 4 Then I answered and said unto the angel that talked with me, "What are these, my Lord?" 5 And the angel answered and said unto me, "These are the four spirits of the heavens, which go forth from standing before the Lord of all the earth."

Animals were first mentioned in death in Ecclesiastes 3:18-21 where it reads: "18 I said in mine heart concerning the estate of the sons of men, that God might manifest them, and that they might see that they themselves are beasts. 19 For that which befalleth the sons of men befalleth beasts; even one thing befalleth them: as the one dieth, so dieth the other; yea, they have all one breath; so that a man hath no preeminence above a beast: for all is vanity. 20 All go unto one place; all are of the dust, and all turn to dust again. 21 Who knoweth the spirit of man that goeth upward, and the spirit of the beast that goeth downward to the earth?

Luke 12:6 "Are not five sparrows sold for two pennies? Yet not one of them is forgotten by God."

The Bible says the animals will exist after the Lord's return – after the Second Coming. In Isaiah 11:6-9 the Bible states: "6 The wolf also shall dwell with the lamb, and the leopard shall lie down with the kid;

and the calf and the young lion and the fatling together; and a little child shall lead them. 7 And the cow and the bear shall feed; their young ones shall lie down together: and the lion shall eat straw like the ox. 8 And the sucking child shall play on the hole of the asp, and the weaned child shall put his hand on the cockatrice' den. 9 They shall not hurt nor destroy in all my holy mountain: for the earth shall be full of the knowledge of the Lord, as the waters cover the sea.

Paul says the spirit of the man is what makes man more intellectually superior to animals. Man was created to possess certain capacities similar to God Himself which enable us to develop skills and learn from the past and future.

Before the great flood, God preserved every species—male and female—on the ark so that all of them would inhabit the land again. We know that God gave them to us for a purpose.

Scientists have proven that animals have intelligence. Whales and Porpoises can converse with other members of their genus through perceptible vernacular. Gorillas can sign simple sentences. Dogs can be trained to perform complex tasks. Elephants are quite intelligent.

But Theologians say that since man is superior to animals that animals cannot be equal.

Perhaps an animal is not equal to us in mentality, but to me that does not mean it does not have a soul. If it has feelings, if it feels pain, if it feels happiness, if it gives freely, if it takes away from you, it has the ability to think, if it has the ability to reason, does that not mean it has a soul?

We know there are horses in heaven. We know God made all animals. It is reasonable to assume that all animals go to heaven. Hopefully not mosquitoes that bite.

The Bible makes it clear in Matthew 7:13-14 that few will make it into heaven. "13 Enter ye in at the strait gate: for wide is the gate, and broad is the way, that leadeth to destruction, and many there be which go in thereat: 14 Because strait is the gate, and narrow is the way, which leadeth unto life, and few there be that find it."

Bible verses that refer to animals are as follows:

Isaiah 11:6-9 - The wolf also shall dwell with the lamb, and the leopard shall lie down with the kid; and the calf and the young lion and the fatling together; and a little child shall lead them.

Revelation 5:13 - And every creature which is in heaven, and on the earth, and under the earth, and such as are in the sea, and all that are in them, heard I saying, Blessing, and honour and glory, and power, [be] unto him that sitteth upon the throne, and unto the Lamb for ever and ever.

Luke 3:6 - And all flesh shall see the salvation of God.

Isaiah 65:25 - The wolf and the lamb shall feed together, and the lion shall eat straw like the bullock: and dust [shall be] the serpent's meat. They shall not hurt nor destroy in all my holy mountain, saith the LORD.

1 Corinthians 2:9 - But as it is written, Eye hath not seen, nor ear heard, neither have entered into the heart of man, the things which God hath prepared for them that love him.

Matthew 10:29 - Are not two sparrows sold for a farthing? and one of them shall not fall on the ground without your Father.

Romans 8:19-22 - For the earnest expectation of the creature waiteth for the manifestation of the sons of God. (Read More...)

Psalms 145:21 - My mouth shall speak the praise of the Lord: and let all flesh bless his holy name for ever and ever.

Genesis 1:25 - And God made the beast of the earth after his kind, and cattle after their kind, and everything that creepeth upon the earth after his kind: and God saw that [it was] good.

Acts 3:19-21 - Repent ye therefore, and be converted, that your sins may be blotted out, when the times of refreshing shall come from the presence of the Lord; (Read More...)

Ecclesiastes 3:1 - To every [thing there is] a season, and a time to every purpose under the heaven:

Proverbs 12:10 - A righteous [man] regardeth the life of his beast: but the tender mercies of the wicked [are] cruel.

Psalms 24:1 - (A Psalm of David.) The earth [is] the Lord's, and the fullness thereof; the world, and they that dwell therein.

Genesis 1:24 - And God said, Let the earth bring forth the living creature after his kind, cattle, and creeping thing, and beast of the earth after his kind: and it was so.

A medium remarked that it is not only cats, dogs, and birds that wait for you in the afterlife. He said that farm animals such as horses and dairy cattle that had been sufficient loved by a human being would wait for their human to come to them in the afterlife.

I believe there is a place in heaven for animals. How about you?

XXI

WHO IS GOD?

God is an eternal, all-knowing, all-powerful, omnipotent, Supreme, loving spirit that created everything that exists. He has limitless grace, mercy and love. God's power over the physical creation is absolute, such that He can manipulate matter, energy, space, and time at will.

Genesis 1:1 states "1. In the beginning God created the heavens and the earth." It gets bigger and better after that.

If you ask "where is God?" That cannot be answered. The Bible says that God cannot be contained within the universe; that God fills both Heaven and Earth, which is a Hebrew idiom to describe the entire universe.

What does God look like? In Genesis 1:27 God said, "27. So God created man in his own image, in the image of God created He Him; male and female created He them." Since we are of human form, that conjures up visions in everyone's mind that God looks like a human the same as the rest of us. But that is not so.

In John 4:24, Jesus told the woman of Samaria, "God is a Spirit: and they that worship Him must worship Him in spirit and in truth."

However, God is able to take on physical form is he wants to interact with humans. God is absolutely holy without any moral or character defects.

When Moses asked God who should he tell the children of Israel who sent Him, God told him to say "I AM" hath sent Me to you.

God spoke directly to many prophets and non-prophets in the old testament. The first record of His communication was with Adam and Eve until He tossed them out of the Garden of Eden. It is not clear how He appeared to them, whether just as a voice, or whether He actually appeared in some form.

Genesis 3:8 states, "8 And they heard the voice of the Lord God walking in the garden in the cool of the day: and Adam and his wife hid themselves from the presence of the Lord God amongst the trees of the garden."

In the First and Second Books of Adam and Eve God usually sent the Angel, Michael to talk to Adam and Eve or to deliver messages. But in the First Book of Adam and Eve God appeared to Adam in some form and talked to him directly. Chapters XXII:1-4 and XXIII 1-5: says: "1. And in that same hour, we heard the archangel Michael blowing with his trumpet and calling to 2. the angels and saying: "Thus saith the Lord, Come with me to paradise and hear the judgment with which I shall judge Adam." 3 And when God appeared in paradise, mounted on the chariot of his cherubim with the angels proceeding before him and singing hymns of praises, all the plants of paradise, both of your father's lot 4 and mine, broke out into flowers. And the throne of God was fixed where the Tree of Life was.

'xxiii. 1 And God called Adam saying, "Adam, where art thou? Can the house be hidden from the presence 2 of its builder?" Then your father answered; "It is not because we think not to be found by thee, Lord, that we hide, but I was afraid because I am naked, and I was ashamed before thy might, 3 (my) Master." God saith to him, "Who showed thee that thou art naked, unless thou hast forsaken my 4 commandment, which I delivered thee to keep (it)." Then Adam called to mind the word which

I spake to him, (saying) "I will make thee secure before God;" and he turned and said to me: "Why 5 hast thou done this?" And I said, "The serpent deceived me."

God spoke to Noah five times over 950 years. He spoke to Abraham eight times over 175 years. He spoke to Isaac two times and He spoke once to Rebekah over 180 years. Then He spoke to Jacob seven times and 1 time directly to Laban over Jacob's lifetime. If it involves God's redemptive plan, He will find the time to talk to you directly.

When Moses wanted to see God, in Exodus 33:20, God said, "20 And He said, thou canst not see my face: for there shall no man see me, and live." God's countenance was so brilliant and dazzling that to look up or at the face of God would kill him. God put Moses in the crest of a rock and shielded him with His hand and passed before Moses and when Moses returned to his people his hair had turned white and his face shone and Moses put a veil on his face.

I had a friend tell me one time she had a difficult time associating a mere man figure as an omnipotent, Supreme Being. I have read many stories about God and how we are connected to God by a cord rather like an umbilical cord. If that is the case, then we are not giving God enough credit. There are 7.4 billion people in the world. That is 7.4 billion cords connected to one God entity at any one time with several hundred thousand beings connected and disconnected daily as some are exchanged through the life and death process. That is what is meant when you hear the phrase "God lives in us." This has to be one gargantuan, enormous, colossal, powerful Supreme Holy Force and that cannot begin to describe Him.

God lives in light so bright we cannot come near it. He is a spirit. When our body dies, our soul will leave our body and become a spirit and if we are ready to go to Heaven, we will live with God. We also become light. We will know love that we have never known previously.

Maybe God just reaches down to our earthly body and unplugs our cord when it is our time to transition and go back to Him.

While we are here on earth we are all perpetual sinners because of Adam and Eve's disobedience in the Garden of Eden. We struggle daily to be the best person we can be and to serve God. We were born and put on this earth for one purpose - to serve God. No one just wants to admit it.

"From these scriptures, we can know that when God appears to a human He takes on the form of a human. Many other scriptures tell how, whenever God appeared to humans, He always had the form and shape, size and features of a normal man. But let's take a closer look.

'God has one face. He talked face to face with Jacob and with Moses (Genesis 32:30, Exodus 33:11, Deuteronomy 34:10). "His eyes are always upon the land He personally cares for" (Deuteronomy 11:12), even as

'His eyes are upon the righteous and His ears are open to their cry (Psalm 34:15).

'Hebrews 4:13 says, "There is no creature hidden from His sight, but all things are naked and open to the eyes of Him to whom we must give account."

'God has a body. Paul tells us that, in the resurrection, our vile, physical bodies will be fashioned like Christ's glorious body (Philippians 3:21). Christ Himself said those who enter the Kingdom will have two eyes, two hands and two feet (Matthew 18:8-9), giving more clear indication of what God looks like.

'God has a mouth, and we are to live by every word that proceeds from it (Matthew 4:4). God spoke to Moses (Numbers 12:8); occasionally He thunders with a mighty voice (Psalm 68:33). Zophar speaks of the lips of God (Job 11:5), and Isaiah tells us that when God becomes angry, "His lips are full of indignation, and His tongue like a devouring fire; His breath is like an over flowing stream" (Isaiah 30:27-28).

'With His voice God laughs at those who try to outwit Him (Psalm 2:4) and at the heathen who plot against Him (Psalm 59:8).

'God has a nose; He smelled the sacrifice Noah offered on the altar (Genesis 8:21), and with a blast from His nostrils He divided the Red Sea (Exodus 15:8).

'God has arms, hands and fingers like we do, not hoofs, claws or paws. God has a mighty arm; strong is His hand, and His right hand is lifted high in glorious strength (Psalm 89:13). The Israelites did not gain possession of the promised land by their own sword or strength, but the right hand and arm of God gained it for them (Psalm 44:3). Jesus Christ now sits at the right hand of the God on high (Hebrews 1:3), and all the host of heaven stand on His right hand and on His left (II Chronicles 18:18).

'With His own fingers God wrote the Ten Commandments on two tablets of stone for Moses (Exodus 31:18, Deuteronomy 9:10), and on two more tables after Moses broke the first set (Deuteronomy 10:1-2). The heavens are the work of God's fingers (Psalm 8:3).

'When God restores all things, the government shall be upon His shoulder (Isaiah 9:6).

'God permitted Moses to see His back as He walked by in His glory (Exodus 33:18, 23), and David speaks of a time when God shook the earth, bowed the heavens and came down when darkness was under His feet (Psalm 18:9). God also has a waist (Ezekiel 1:27).

'Jesus Christ said, "He who has seen Me has seen the Father" (John 14:9), indicating that both God the Father and Christ have the same form and shape, and undoubtedly much the same looks and features."

http://www.hwalibrary.com/cgi-bin/get/hwa.cgi?action= getmagazine&InfoID=1328719734

When Ezekiel went to Heaven he described God as follows in Ezekiel 1:26: "And above the firmament that was over their heads was the likeness of a throne, as the appearance of a sapphire stone: and upon the likeness of the throne was the likeness as the appearance of a man above upon it. 27. And I saw as the colour of amber, as the appearance of fire round about within it, from the appearance of his loins even upward, and from the appearance of his loins even downward, I saw as it were the appearance of fire, and it had brightness round about. 28 As the appearance of the bow that is in the cloud in the day of rain, so was the appearance of the brightness round about. This was the appearance of the likeness of the glory of the Lord. And when I saw it, I fell upon my face, and I heard a voice of one that spake."

Another description was given by John in Revelation 1:14-17 which states: "14. His head and his hairs were white like wool, as white as snow; and His eyes were as a flame of fire; 15 And His feet like unto fine brass, as if they burned in a furnace; and His voice as the sound of many waters. 16 And He had in his right hand seven stars: and out of his mouth went a sharp two-edged sword: and His countenance was as the sun shineth in His strength. 17 And when I saw Him, I fell at His feet as dead. And He laid his right hand upon me, saying unto me, Fear not; I am the first and the last:"

No one of today's world knows what God looks like, or what Jesus looks like. Some that have had near-death experiences believe they have seen Jesus. Perhaps they have. Knowing what I do about the other dimension, I believe that is possible. Knowing what I do about religion, I believe that is possible. They just describe Him as pure love. But for those of us that by the grace of God are to make it into Heaven one day, we will then find out what God looks like as we praise Him.

XXII

YOU CAN KNOW YOU ARE GOING TO HEAVEN

In the book of Romans, Chapter 10, verse 9, the Bible says "That if thou shalt confess with thy mouth the Lord Jesus, and shalt believe in thine heart that God hath raised Him from the dead, thou shalt be saved.

Sounds simple, doesn't it? It is. If you are sincere and want to turn your life over to Jesus, just kneel before our Lord and say this prayer.

"Dear Lord Jesus, I acknowledge to You that I am a sinner, and I am sorry for my sins and the life that I have lived; I need Your forgiveness.

'I believe that You shed Your precious blood on the cross at Calvary and died for my sins, and I am now willing to turn from my sin.

'You said in Your Holy Word, Romans 10:9 that if we confess the Lord our God and believe in our hearts that God raised Jesus from the dead, we shall be saved.

'Right now, I confess Jesus as the Lord of my soul. With my heart, I believe that God raised Jesus from the dead. This very moment I accept

Jesus Christ as my own personal Savior and according to His Word, right now I am saved.

'Thank you, Jesus for your unlimited grace which has saved me from my sins. I thank You, Jesus, that Your grace never leads to license, but rather it always leads to repentance. Therefore, Lord Jesus transform my life so that I may bring glory and honor to You alone and not to myself.

'Thank you, Jesus for dying for me and giving me eternal life. Amen."

We were put in this world to serve God. It is not about us; it is all about God. It is about living our life for God. For having a desire to do His will, not our will. For having a desire to help others. Our rewards come in the afterlife. When you give your life to Jesus you will find not only peace and happiness in this life but peace and love for eternity.

I wasn't even a teenager when I became a Christian. Our family was walking home from church and I remember I was so happy that I skipped all the way home. I had this joy inside of me that I have never been able to duplicate by any other experience. All I wanted to do was to please God. Until such time as I left home, I worked with other young people in the church and I taught Sunday School for the little ones and did what I could in what I considered working for God.

I do hope in some way you will realize that there is life after death before it is too late and that you will seek out God in your life. He is real and He loves you. He is waiting for you to call upon Him.

I would rather live my life believing there is a God and find out there is not a God than live my life believing there is not a God and find out there is one.

THE END
Is it?

www.ingramcontent.com/pod-product-compliance
Lightning Source LLC
Chambersburg PA
CBHW052044090426
42739CB00010B/2046